The Gender Equality Debate

Editor: Tracy Biram

Volume 364

Independence Educational Publishers

First published by Independence Educational Publishers
The Studio, High Green
Great Shelford
Cambridge CB22 5EG
England

Copyright

Photocopy licence

ISBN-13: 978 1 86168 821 7

Printed in Great Britain

Zenith Print Group

Contents

Chapter 1: Gender Equality Overview

Chapter 2: Stereotypes

Introduction

The Gender Equality Debate is Volume 364 in the ***ISSUES*** series. The aim of the series is to offer current, diverse information about important issues in our world, from a UK perspective.

ABOUT THE GENDER EQUALITY DEBATE

Have we finally achieved gender equality, or do we still have a long way to go? This book explores the negative impact gender-based inequalities can have on both males and females. We take a look at issues such as FGM, the gender pay gap, harmful stereotypes and toxic masculinity. We also consider how society is changing to address these issues.

OUR SOURCES

Titles in the ***ISSUES*** series are designed to function as educational resource books, providing a balanced overview of a specific subject.

The information in our books is comprised of facts, articles and opinions from many different sources, including:

- Newspaper reports and opinion pieces
- Website factsheets
- Magazine and journal articles
- Statistics and surveys
- Government reports
- Literature from special interest groups.

A NOTE ON CRITICAL EVALUATION

Because the information reprinted here is from a number of different sources, readers should bear in mind the origin of the text and whether the source is likely to have a particular bias when presenting information (or when conducting their research). It is hoped that, as you read about the many aspects of the issues explored in this book, you will critically evaluate the information presented.

It is important that you decide whether you are being presented with facts or opinions. Does the writer give a biased or unbiased report? If an opinion is being expressed, do you agree with the writer? Is there potential bias to the 'facts' or statistics behind an article?

ACTIVITIES

In the back of this book, you will find a selection of assignments designed to help you engage with the articles you have been reading and to explore your own opinions. Some tasks will take longer than others and there is a mixture of design, writing and research-based activities that you can complete alone or in a group.

FURTHER RESEARCH

At the end of each article we have listed its source and a website that you can visit if you would like to conduct your own research. Please remember to critically evaluate any sources that you consult and consider whether the information you are viewing is accurate and unbiased.

Useful Websites

www.asa.org.uk
www.broadcastnow.co.uk
www.theconversation.com
www.designweek.co.uk
www.ecnmy.org
www.fawcettsociety.org.uk
www.theguardian.com
www.independent.co.uk
www.inews.co.uk
www.news-decoder.com
www.ohchr.org
www.ons.gov.uk
www.telegraph.co.uk
www.understandingsociety.ac.uk
www.unwomen.org
www.weforum.org
www.yougov.co.uk

7 surprising and outrageous stats about gender inequality

By Kate Whiting

Around the world, the achievements of women are being celebrated on International Women's Day, which began back in 1911. But the day also highlights the work that remains to be done in order to achieve gender parity.

The theme for this year is #BalanceforBetter – encapsulating the idea that a gender balanced world benefits everyone, economically and socially. And it's up to everyone, men and women, to make it happen.

As the following statistics show, there are huge differences in the types of inequality faced by women in different parts of the world – from cultural representation, to domestic burdens and child marriage. But through collective action and shared ownership, change is possible.

1. Women are 47% more likely to suffer severe injuries in car crashes because safety features are designed for men

In their 2011 study of more than 45,000 crash victims over 11 years, researchers from the University of Virginia found women drivers were much more likely to be injured in a crash than men.

They said this was because car safety features had been designed for men. The positioning of head restraints, as well as women's shorter height, different neck strength and musculature, as well as their preferred seating position, meant they were more susceptible to injury.

2. 33,000 girls become child brides every day

Globally, 12 million girls each year get married before the age of 18 – roughly 33,000 every day, or one every two seconds. There are some 650 million women alive today who were child brides.

The reasons behind it vary between communities, but it's often because girls are not valued as highly as boys and marrying them off at a young age transfers the 'economic burden' to another family.

3. Women in rural parts of Africa spend 40 billion hours a year collecting water

In rural parts of sub-Saharan Africa, a lack of services and infrastructure, combined with an expectation of household duties and limited employment opportunities for women, means they shoulder an unequal burden of gathering water and wood for their families.

Average hours per week spent fetching wood and water in rural areas of selected sub-Saharan African countries

	Guinea (2002–03)	Madagascar (2001)	Malawi (2004)	Sierra Leone (2003–04)
women	5.7	4.7	9.1	7.3
men	2.3	4.1	1.1	4.5
girls	4.1	5.1	4.3	7.7
boys	4.0	4.7	1.4	7.1

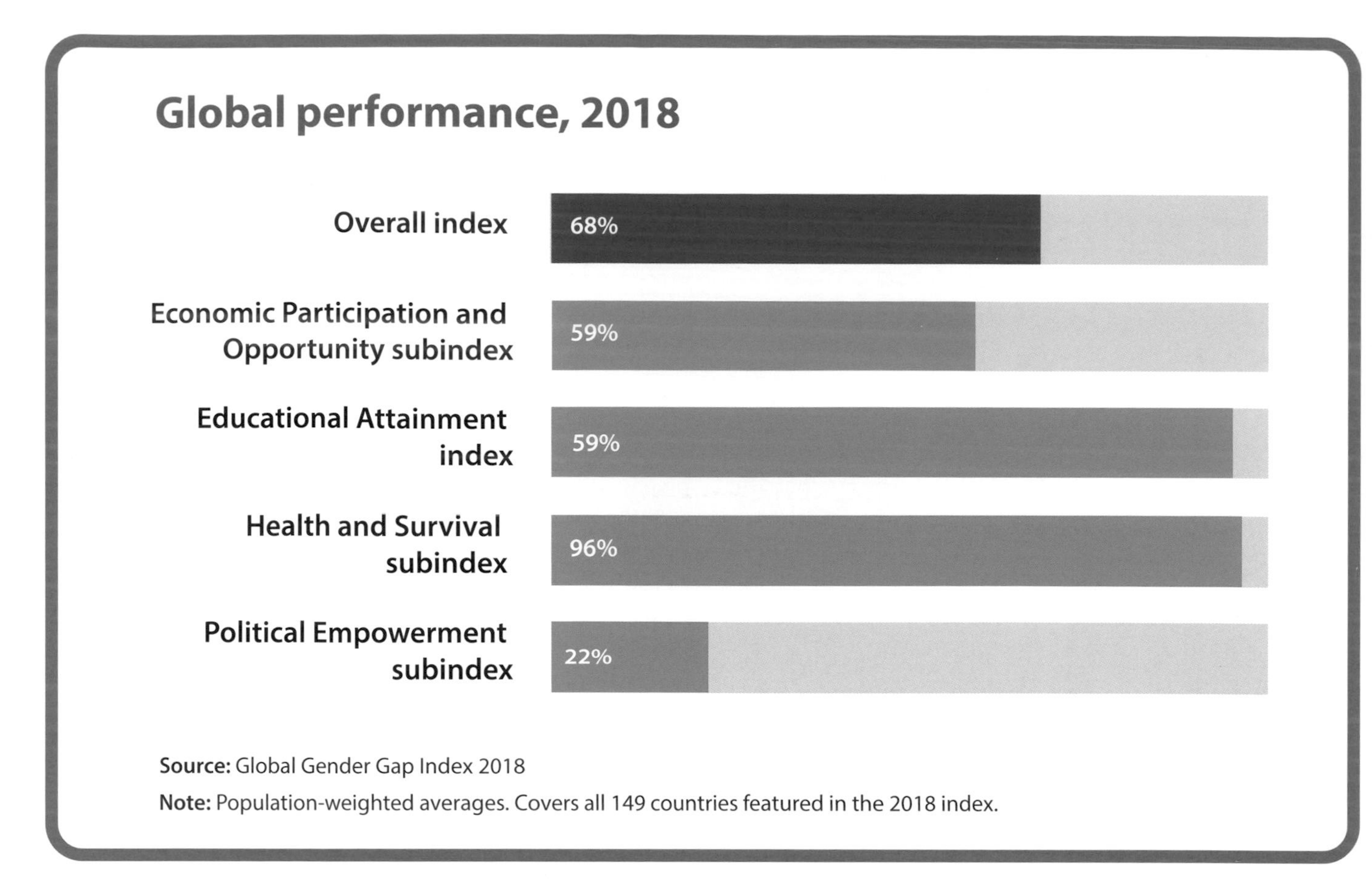

Source: Global Gender Gap Index 2018

Note: Population-weighted averages. Covers all 149 countries featured in the 2018 index.

According to the UN, collectively these women spend 40 billion hours a year collecting water.

4. It will take 108 years to close the gender gap

At the current rate of progress, it will take another 108 years to reach gender parity, according to the World Economic Forum's most recent *Global Gender Gap Report*.

Across the 106 countries covered since the first edition of the report, the biggest gaps to close are in the economic and political empowerment dimensions, which will take 202 and 107 years to close, respectively.

5. Only 6 countries give women equal legal work rights as men

The World Bank's recent Women, Business and the Law report measured gender discrimination in 187 countries.

It found that only Belgium, Denmark, France, Latvia, Luxembourg and Sweden scored full marks on eight indicators – from receiving a pension to freedom of movement – influencing economic decisions women make during their careers.

A typical economy only gives women three-quarters the rights of men in the measured areas.

6. 22% of AI professionals are women – and it could be down to lack of confidence

According to the Forum's *Global Gender Gap Report*, only 22% of the world's AI professionals are female, compared with 78% who are male. This accounts for a gender gap of 72% yet to close – and reflects the broader STEM skills gap.

In 2012, just 14% of women starting university in OECD countries chose science-related subjects, compared with 39% of men.

A 2015 PISA report found even high-achieving girls underachieved when they were asked to 'think like scientists'. Girls were less confident at solving science and maths problems and reported higher levels of anxiety towards maths.

In a study of students at Cornell University in 2003, psychologists found that women rated their scientific abilities lower than men, even though they performed roughly the same in a quiz.

The researchers said: "Women might disproportionately avoid scientific pursuits because their self-views lead them to mischaracterize how well they are objectively doing on any given scientific task."

7. For every female film character, there are 2.24 men

The Geena Davis Institute analysed 120 theatrical releases between 2010 and 2013 in ten countries – and found that of the 5,799 speaking or named characters, less than a third (30.9%) were female and more than a third (69.1%) were male.

8 March 2019

To achieve gender equality, we must first tackle our unconscious biases

An article from **The Conversation.**

THE CONVERSATION

By Beatrice Alba, Research Fellow, La Trobe University

People often argue that most Western societies have achieved gender equality – women have all the same legal rights as men, and workplace discrimination based on gender is illegal. Despite this, feminists continue to argue that the battle for gender equality is not yet won.

So what do we mean when we talk about gender equality, and how will we know when we have it?

What does the evidence tell us?

There is evidence of widespread prejudice against women and girls from decades of psychological research. For instance, an experiment was conducted in which participants watched an entrepreneurial pitch video of images relating to a new venture, narrated by the voice of the entrepreneur. Participants were randomly assigned to a group in which either a male or female voice narrated the pitch, which was otherwise identical. When a male voice pitched the venture, 68% of participants thought it was worthy of funding, compared to only 32% when pitched by a female voice.

Such effects occur even when gender is presented only on paper. In an experiment in which participants were asked to rate an applicant for a laboratory manager position, an identical application was provided in two separate conditions. However, in each condition, the application was randomly assigned as belonging to either 'John' or 'Jennifer'. Participants who were led to believe the applicant was male rated them as more competent and hireable, as well as offering them a higher starting salary and more career mentoring.

Even children show this gender bias. One study asked children to guess whether a 'really, really smart' protagonist in a story was a man or a woman. By the age of six, girls were less likely to guess that the protagonist was a woman than boys were to guess that the protagonist was a man.

This scientific evidence demonstrates that people do in fact discriminate based on gender, despite denials that gender inequality persists in modern societies. This research demonstrates that even when all else is equal, women are at a disadvantage to men in many domains. This might be because men are perceived as being more capable in general, even in the absence of evidence to suggest superior skills.

Equal does not mean identical

One might object that there are meaningful differences between males and females, and these in turn are the source of gender inequality. Some believe that equality is the wrong word to use, because males and females can't be equal if they are different.

But when feminists refer to gender equality, we are not arguing that males and females are identical or indistinguishable on all behaviour, preferences and abilities. Nor does it mean all gender differences must be eliminated, or that we must have equal gender representation in every field.

For instance, there are many more male firefighters than female firefighters. Part of this is likely due to gender differences in work preferences. But it is also partly due to the physical strength tests used in recruiting firefighters. These include being able to lift a 72kg mannequin and drag it for 45 metres. Many fit men can achieve this feat, but substantially fewer fit women can.

Even in the absence of gender discrimination, we might always have fewer female firefighters simply because of such physical requirements. But as long as these requirements are reasonable for the job and no woman is excluded because she is a woman, then gender discrimination is not a problem. Gender equality doesn't mean we must have a 50:50 balance of men and women in every profession purely for the sake of equal representation.

Equality or equity?

Gender equality also does not mean that males and females must always be treated the same. Given the existence of biological sex differences, it is reasonable for males and females to have different legal rights in some instances. For example, only females can ever require maternity leave specifically for pregnancy and birth.

In cases such as these, what is required is not equal treatment, but equitable treatment. Equity means recognising that differences in ability mean that fairness often requires treating people differently so that they can achieve the same outcome. At times equity is necessary to achieve gender equality, but there are many instances where this is not the case.

Most of the time, women and girls are at no inherent disadvantage due to a lack of ability that warrants differential treatment. Gender equality can often be achieved just by holding everyone to the same standard. The problem, as highlighted by the evidence reviewed above, is the irrational gender bias that women and girls are routinely subjected to.

The purpose of affirmative action policies to increase female representation is to counteract systemic discrimination against women. Affirmative action creates gender equity by overcoming the barriers women face simply because of their gender. If we can eliminate this gender-based discrimination, no such action will be necessary.

Achieving gender equality

So if gender equality does not mean that males and females must be identical or always require the same treatment in order to achieve fairness, what does it mean?

Gender equality is seeing males and females as being of equal status and value. It is judging a person based on their merit, and not viewing them as inferior or superior purely based on their gender.

Unfortunately, the evidence reviewed above suggests this prejudice is still widespread, and we often aren't aware of our own biases. We cannot say that we have gender equality until this prejudice is overcome and we have eliminated the irrational bias that people have against somebody just because they are female.

Equal rights are not enough. Inequality exists in our minds, in our biases and prejudices, and that remains to be fixed.

7 March 2018

Gender equality: a global human rights crisis

Gender equality is not only a fundamental human right but a foundation for peace and prosperity. Feminists fight not just for women, but all humans.

By Jaymee Hick

When I was six years old, I was called bossy for wanting to be the leader in playground games.

When I was nine years old, my brother was bluntly told, 'Dancing isn't for boys,' after he watched my ballet rehearsals.

When I was 10 years old, corporate giants decided to sexualise my body as I was forced into a world of curves and skin exposure.

When I was 12 years old, I was labelled a 'know-it-all' when I won the annual class academic prize. My male counterpart was championed as a 'genius'.

When I was 13 years old, I witnessed my father being mocked by friends because he was the cook in our family.

When I was 14 years old, I walked through a park as a male stranger yelled out his car window to label me to the world as a 'cheeky slut'.

When I was 17 years old, I watched male friends suffocate under a curtain of anxiety, with no way visible to unveil themselves and ask for help.

When I was 18 years old, I held my best friend in my arms and watched her spirit shatter into a million pieces, asking why that boy decided he would take her body without its owner's permission.

> *"Equality is not the advancing of women and tearing down of men."*

Five days ago, someone texted me a joke: 'How many feminists does it take to change a light bulb?'

They believed the punch line – 'It doesn't matter. They can't change anything.' – would be an entertaining way to provoke me.

Well, it did.

Yes, I mentioned that dirty word. Feminism.

Type the word into a Google search bar, and here's the definition you get: 'The advocacy of women's rights on the basis of the equality of the sexes.'

Our world today seems only to want to acknowledge the first part of that definition.

However, it's the second part, the part most people forget about when they decide to presumptuously label 'feminists' as 'crazy man-haters', that screams for attention. Because in its most fundamental and simple translation into everyday life, it calls for gender equality.

As the third goal of the United Nations Millennium Development Goals, gender equality is seen not only

Yet there are some problems that both developed and developing nations share.

Human trafficking, sexual and domestic violence, wage gap and under-representation in the workplace and government stand in the way of full equality.

According to the *Global Gender Gap Report 2017*, at our current rate it will take 217 years to close the gender gap in the economic sphere.

Today, men hold more than eight of every ten seats in the US Congress and make up the majority of mayors and governors. These are the people with the power to implement tangible change in our world.

But if our world's population is not fairly represented, does this not undermine the very essence of our liberal democracy?

"Gender equality is a human right."

Significantly, both men and women share some common problems.

Domestic abuse and violence affect one in three women throughout their lifetime, and one in four men.

Constant societal pressure to fit the conventional mould of gender stereotypes is a shared challenge. We need to push the conversation to allow for men to be not only powerful, but emotionally open, and for women to be not only emotionally open, but powerful.

as a fundamental human right, but also as a 'necessary foundation for a peaceful, prosperous and sustainable world'.

Equality. Not the advancing of women and tearing down of men. But our collective recognition that both sexes have problems that unite them and that need to be fairly addressed.

"How can we move forward without the voices of 62 million people?"

Whilst most women in developed nations have the privilege of affordable and accessible education, the United Nations Foundation estimates that 62 million girls worldwide are denied this basic human right.

It's hard to comprehend what a lack of education must feel like when we have grown up in a society where education equality is the norm. But the consequences of it are dire.

It not only means illiteracy and an inability to apply basic numerical concepts, but robs girls of opportunities for self-empowerment. And without such empowerment, how do we expect to move forward in our world without the voices of 62 million people?

As Emma Watson asserted in an inspiring speech to the UN in 2014: 'It is time that we all perceive gender on a spectrum instead of two sets of opposing ideals.'

Feminism may be a complex term in today's whirlwind of conflicting voices and long entrenched connotations. But gender equality is the ideal for which we must strive. As actress Frieda Pinto said, 'Gender equality is a human right, not a female fight.'

20 December 2017

Statement: Take action to eliminate female genital mutilation by 2030

In a joint statement for the International Day of Zero Tolerance for Female Genital Mutilation, UN Women Executive Director Phumzile Mlambo Ngcuka, UNFPA Executive Director Natalia Kanem, and UNICEF Executive Director Henrietta H. Fore, reaffirm their commitment to end this violation of human rights.

Mary Oloiparuni was 13 when she was mutilated. Restrained in a doorway early one morning in her home, she was cut, bled profusely and experienced agonising pain. The scarring she endured then continues to cause her pain today, 19 years later. It has made giving birth to each of her five children an excruciating and harrowing experience.

Mary is not alone. At least 200 million girls and women alive today have had their genitals mutilated – suffering one of the most inhuman acts of gender-based violence in the world.

On the International Day of Zero Tolerance for Female Genital Mutilation, we reaffirm our commitment to end this violation of human rights, so that the tens of millions of girls who are still at risk of being mutilated by 2030 do not experience the same suffering as Mary.

This effort is especially critical because female genital mutilation leads to long-term physical, psychological and social consequences. It violates women's rights to sexual and reproductive health, physical integrity, non-discrimination and freedom from cruel or degrading treatment. It is also a violation of medical ethics: female genital mutilation is never safe, no matter who carries it out or how clean the venue is.

Because female genital mutilation is a form of gender-based violence, we cannot address it in isolation from other forms of violence against women and girls, or other harmful practices such as early and forced marriages. To end female genital mutilation, we have to tackle the root causes of gender inequality and work for women's social and economic empowerment.

In 2015, world leaders overwhelmingly backed the elimination of female genital mutilation as one of the targets in the 2030 Agenda for Sustainable Development. This is an achievable goal, and we must act now to translate that political commitment into action.

At the national level, we need new policies and legislation protecting the rights of girls and women to live free from violence and discrimination. Governments in countries where female genital mutilation is prevalent should also develop national action plans to end the practice. To be effective, their plans must include budget lines dedicated to comprehensive sexual and reproductive health, education, social welfare and legal services.

At the regional level, we need institutions and economic communities to work together, preventing the movement of girls and women across borders when the purpose is to get them into countries with less restrictive female genital mutilation laws.

Locally, we need religious leaders to strike down myths that female genital mutilation has a basis in religion. Because societal pressures often drive the practice, individuals and families need more information about the benefits of abandoning it.

Public pledges to abandon female genital mutilation – particularly pledges by entire communities – are an effective model of collective commitment. But public pledges must be paired with comprehensive strategies for challenging the social norms, practices and behaviours that condone female genital mutilation. Testimonials by survivors like Mary also help to build understanding of the practice's grim reality and long-lasting impact on women's lives. Advocacy campaigns and social media can amplify the message that ending female genital mutilation saves and improves lives.

Thanks to the collective action of governments, civil society, communities and individuals, female genital mutilation is in decline. But we are not aiming for fewer cases of this practice. We are insisting on zero.

4 February 2019

www.unwomen.org

Majority of Britons think gender equality has yet to be reached in seven key areas

Each year International Women's Day (IWD) highlights the social, economic, cultural and political achievements of women across the world. This year's celebration specifically calls for an acceleration of gender equality.

By Tanya Abraham, Associate Director for the Political Team

With this in mind, YouGov asked Brits whether they think equality has been achieved or whether further progress is needed in eight different areas, ranging from workplace representation to equal household responsibilities.

More needs to be done in all areas but equal pay is the most pressing

Across all fields, a majority think that more needs to be done; the largest figure was the 71% who feel that there's still some way to go in achieving equal gender pay in Britain. Four in five (80%) women have this opinion compared to 62% of men. In addition, older people are more likely to think more action is required (78% of those aged 65 and over, compared to 59% of 18– to 24–year–olds).

When asked whether they felt equal gender pay had been achieved for themselves personally, 40% of women said progress was still required in this area, compared to 27% of men. A plurality of Londoners (42%) also appear to want more to be done compared to a third or less in other regions of Britain.

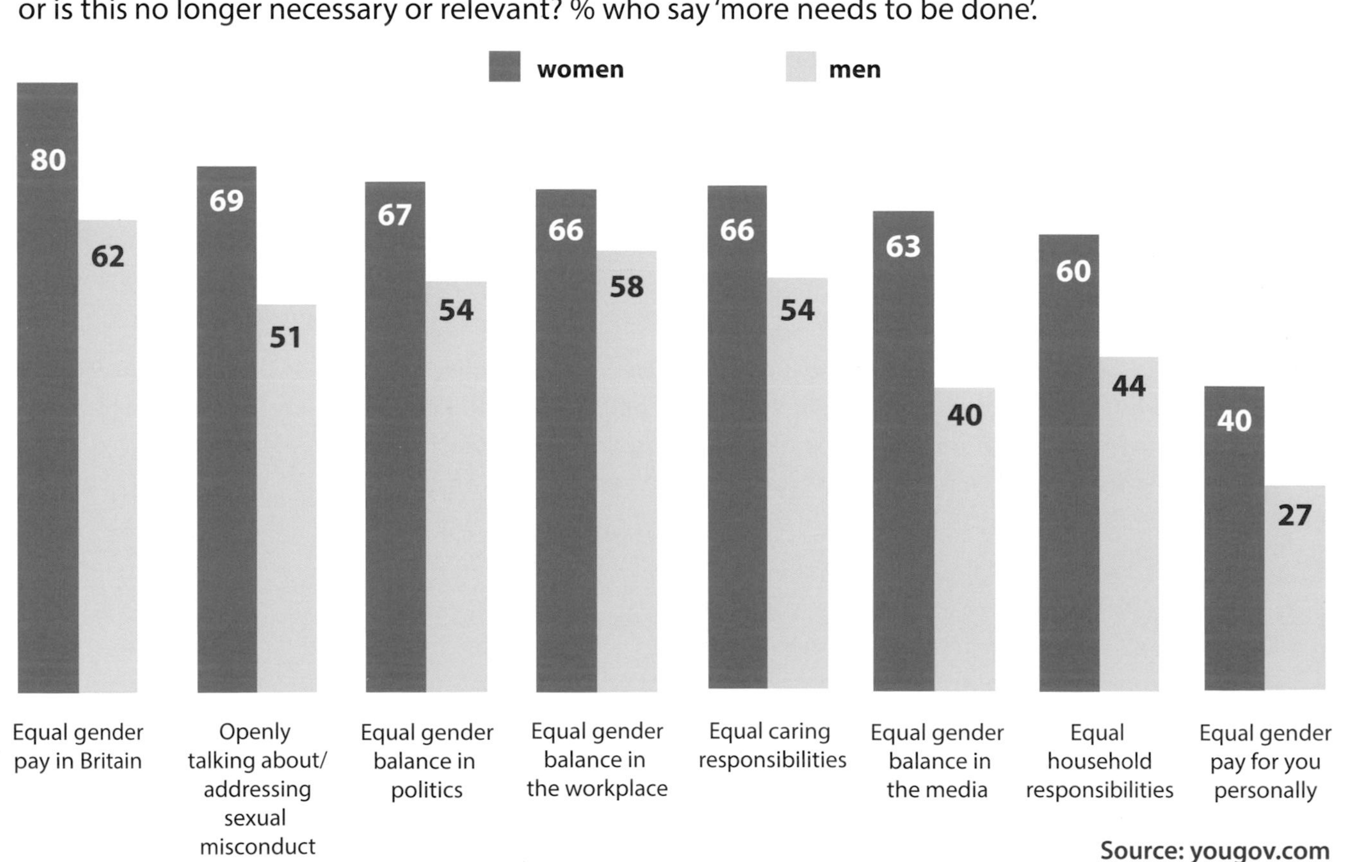

How many women and men feel that gender equality has already been achieved?

Do you think that each of the following areas have been achieved or should more be done, or is this no longer necessary or relevant? % who say 'This has been achieved'.

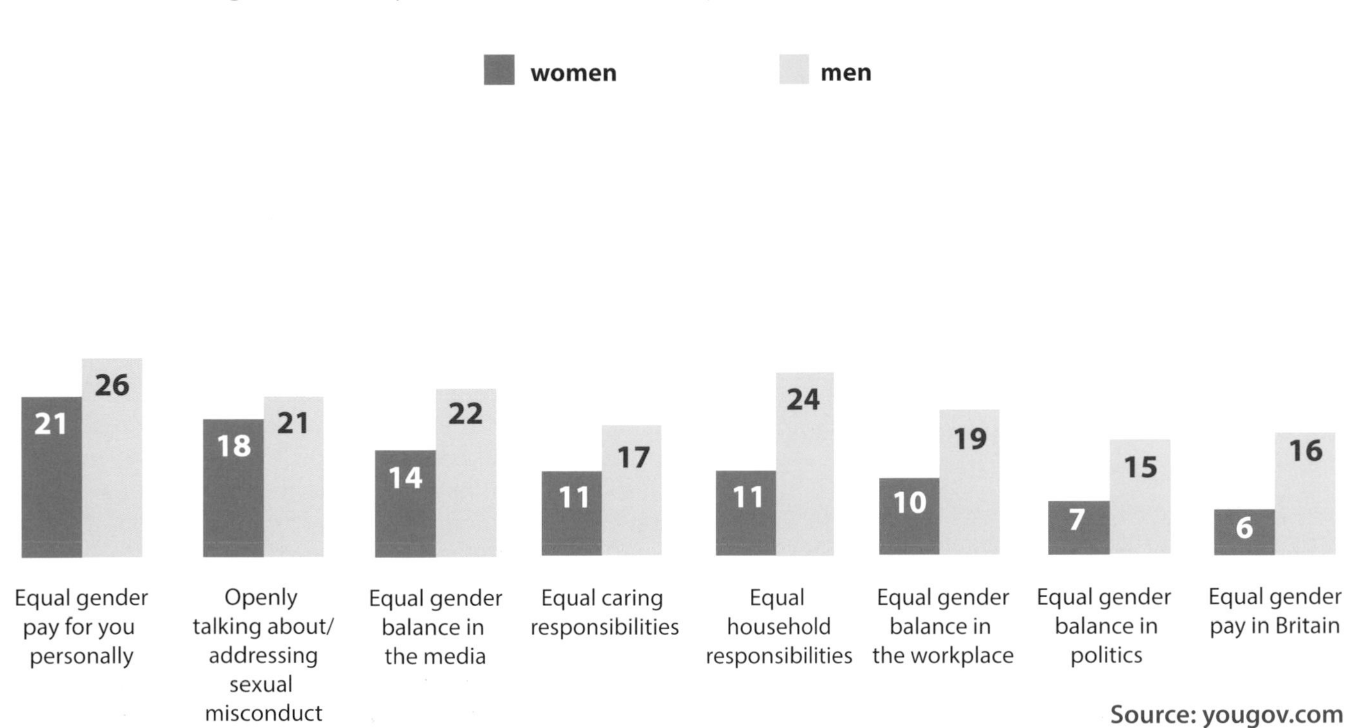

Source: yougov.com

The public sphere

When it comes to public figures, half of Brits (53%) think more must be done to address the equal gender balance in the media, while 18% think balance has been achieved.

Women are more likely than men to think more work is required by 62% to 47%.

Even more Britons (61%) think progress is still needed to reach gender parity in British politics, including two-thirds of women (67%) and a majority of men (54%).

A similar proportion (60%) say further action is required in order to reach an equal gender balance in the workplace, with women again substantially more likely to hold this view than men (69% versus 51%).

The home front

Even at home, gender equality is still lacking. The majority of Brits think that more needs to be done when it comes to equal caring responsibilities (60%) and equal household responsibilities (52%). In fact, the single biggest difference in attitudes between men and women was over the need for more action when it comes to household duties – 63% of women, compared to 40% of men.

Approaching sexual misconduct

While the #MeToo movement has thrust sexual harassment into the public conversation these last 18 months, three in five Brits (62%) still think more needs to be done when it comes to openly talking about or addressing sexual misconduct. Two in three women (66%) would like to see more action compared to 58% of men.

Notably, this area also has the smallest proportion of people (5%) who think that addressing misconduct is no longer relevant or necessary.

What's closest to being achieved?

Only 23% of Britons felt that equal gender pay for themselves had been achieved, and this was the highest figure for any of the eight categories. This is also notably the only personal category of the eight – the rest all referred to society or industries in general, and for these only between 11% and 19% of people (and just between 6% and 18% of women) feel that gender equality has been achieved.

3–4 March 2019

www.yougov.co.uk

How far have women's rights advanced in a century?

By Mark Molloy

This year marks the centenary of women gaining the right to vote in Great Britain and Ireland. But while the feminist movement has made monumental strides since, the campaign for equality still continues today.

The watershed moment for the British women's suffrage movement, came 100 years ago when the Representation of the People Act was given Royal Assent from George V on 6 February 1918, giving approximately 8.4 million women the vote.

Introducing the bill against the backdrop of a united country fighting the First World War, the Home Secretary George Cave said: 'War by all classes of our countrymen has brought us nearer together, has opened men's eyes, and removed misunderstandings on all sides.

'It has made it, I think, impossible that ever again, at all events in the lifetime of the present generation, there should be a revival of the old class feeling which was responsible for so much, and, among other things, for the exclusion for a period, of so many of our population from the class of electors. I think I need say no more to justify this extension of the franchise.'

1918 vs 2018 | Things women were prevented from doing by law a century ago

- Applying for a credit card or loan in their own name
- Working in the legal profession and civil service
- Inheriting and bequeathing property on the same terms as men
- Claiming equal pay for doing the same work as men
- Prosecuting a spouse for rape

It meant women over the age of 30, who met specific property qualifications, could vote for the first time – however,it would take another decade for women over 21 to be given the same voting rights as men.

The 1918 Act, championed by suffrage pioneer Millicent Fawcett and suffragette leaders the Pankhursts, is considered a pivotal moment for women's rights and helped lay the foundations for progress towards greater political, social and economic equality.

But, a century later, women still face gender equality barriers and prejudice, as highlighted by the gender pay gap, Time's Up movement and countless examples of everyday sexism. The Fawcett Society says there is still much progress to be made.

'We have come a long way since some women first got the vote, but there is so much more that needs to be done,' chief executive Sam Smethers told *The Telegraph*.

'As the #metoo movement and the Presidents Club scandal shows, the law around sexual harassment must be strengthened to cover harassment from customers, clients and co-workers, and we must widen access to justice.

'As the BBC pay scandal shows, the law must change so that more women can exercise their right to equal pay and we must place greater emphasis on the organisation's responsibility to prevent discrimination. And as we are still stuck at only a third women MPs, all political parties must set out clear action plans to get more women in.'

According to a 2017 report by the World Economic Forum, it could still take another 100 years before the global equality gap between men and women disappears entirely.

While there is still significant progress to be made, the achievements and evolution of the feminist movement and the sea-change in attitudes towards women's rights over the past century will be celebrated with commemorative events around the country in 2018.

The fight for women's suffrage

During the 19th century, women held an inferior position to men in British society, both socially and legally.

Before 1870, married women were required to relinquish all property and earnings to their husbands, effectively giving them the same legal status as an insane person or a criminal. It would be another 120 years before rape within marriage would be made a criminal offence.

Women were also excluded from being elected onto borough or county councils or as an MP. They were also prevented from accessing higher education until 1878.

The two sexes 'inhabited what Victorians thought of as separate spheres, only coming together at breakfast and again at dinner,' explains Professor Kathryn Hughes, an expert in Victorian history.

Support for the movement grows

In 1866, the London Society for Women's Suffrage, presented a petition to Parliament asking for women to be granted the vote.

'When Millicent Fawcett and other campaigners were handing over their petition for women's suffrage to Parliament, women had few legal rights,' say the Fawcett Society.

Landmark dates for women

1867
National Society for Women's Suffrage is formed; Lydia Becker becomes secretary of the Manchester Society

1870
Married Women's Property Act comes into effect, allowing married women to own property

1903
Emmeline Pankhurst founds the Women's Social and Political Union (WSPU), which later becomes known as the suffragette movement

1905
Militant campaign begins: Christabel Pankhurst and Annie Kenney are arrested for assault and imprisoned

1907
The Women's Freedom League (WFL) emerges from the WSPU, rejecting the dominance of the Pankhursts

1908
Mass rally in London. Between 300,000 and 500,000 activists gather in Hyde Park and windows are smashed in Downing Street

1909
Start of suffragette hunger strikes and force-feeding in prison

1910
On what became known as Black Friday, women protest at Westminster as the Conciliation Bill (which would have given them the vote) fails to pass. 115 women are arrested and two die

1913
Emily Wilding Davison throws herself under the King's horse; the 'Cat and Mouse' Act means hunger strikers are temporarily released from prison so they don't die in police custody

1918
Representation of the People Act grants women over 30 the right to vote (and men over 21 the same right)

1928
Women over 21 are given equal voting rights with men

1929
Margaret Bondfield becomes the first woman cabinet minister

1956
Legal reforms require equal pay for women teachers and civil servants

1961
Contraception (including the Pill) becomes available for married women on the NHS

1967
The Abortion Act decriminalises abortion in Britain on certain grounds

1970
The Equal Pay Act, prohibiting any less favourable treatment between men and women in terms of pay, becomes law

1979
Margaret Thatcher becomes Britain's first female prime minister

1991
Rape within marriage is made a crime

2018
Under equal pay legislation, by 4 April this year employers with more than 250 staff are required to report salary figures for men and women

'They could not vote in national elections, had no access to higher education, were subject to state endorsed violence from their husbands and were the property of men, usually their fathers or husbands.

'150 years later we have seen our society transformed.'

Support for the movement had grown substantially by 1888, with 1,400 women protesting against poor wages and working conditions at a factory in London's East End.

20 years later, 300,000 to 500,000 activists gathered at a rally in Hyde Park, London, in support of women's suffrage.

'From the point of view of numbers, yesterday's women's suffrage demonstration in Hyde Park will rank among the biggest gatherings ever made in the metropolis,' *The Daily Telegraph* reported.

'Christabel Pankhurst, speaking with pride of the success of the huge gathering, expressed the hope that this would be the last meeting of this kind and that it would convince the Government that public opinion demanded that the Parliamentary vote should be given to women.'

In 1913, suffragette Emily Davison gave her life in the fight for women's rights when she was trampled under George V's horse after running onto the track at the Epsom Derby, the most famous act of an increasingly militant campaign.

Women finally gained the vote in 1918, with the Act paving the way for universal suffrage ten years later and far-reaching equal rights legislation introduced over the next 100 years, with progress in education, work, violence against women and at home.

In the workplace

The Sex Discrimination Removal Act 1919 meant women could no longer be disqualified from certain professions on the grounds of sex.

It gave women access to the legal profession and accountancy for the first time and meant they could also hold any civil or judicial office or post.

Property

In 1922, the Law of Property Act allowed both husband and wife to inherit property equally, legislation passed four years later meant women could hold and dispose of property on the same terms as men.

Before 1870, women were required to give up all property rights and money earned to their husbands upon marriage. The Married Women's Property Act gave wives control of their own possessions and meant any money which a woman earned would be treated as her own property.

Women become 'people'

In 1929, women became 'persons' in their own right under Canadian law following a ruling by the Privy Council.

Canadian Emily Murphy, the first female magistrate in the British Empire, and four others, led the fight after lawyers challenged her right to pass sentence, arguing that as a woman she was not qualified to sit in the Senate of Canada.

A plaque created in their honour in the chamber reads: 'To further the cause of womankind these five outstanding pioneer women caused steps to be taken resulting in the recognition by the Privy Council of women as persons eligible for appointment to the Senate of Canada.'

Equal pay

A strike by 187 female workers at a Ford car factory in Dagenham in 1968 is cited as being instrumental in the passing of the 1970 Equal Pay Act.

The machinists walked out and went on strike for three weeks in protest against their male colleagues earning 15 per cent more than them.

Former Labour Party MP Shirley Summerskill said the women played a 'very significant part in the history of the struggle for equal pay'.

Discrimination

The Sex Discrimination Act 1975 made it illegal to discriminate against women in work, education and training. It also meant women could apply for a credit card or loan in their own name.

The Equality Act 2010 would eventually replace a number of different anti-discrimination laws.

Equal pay for equal work

The Equal Pay (Amendment) Act 1983 allowed women to be paid the same as men for work of equal value.

Marital rape

It was not until 1991 that the House of Lords made rape in marriage a criminal offence in the UK.

Women's rights today

Last year's women's march and protests were attended by more than five million people in 81 countries worldwide. It was the largest single-day protest in US history.

In a statement before this year's march, the organisers said: 'We are coming together to pledge that we are going to make change in big and small ways. We will stand side by side, once again, in solidarity with our sisters, brothers and siblings around the world. Together we are strong and if we all work for a better world then time is really up for oppressors of women.'

6 February 2018

School trousers or skirts for all: 'children should experience equality'

As John Lewis removes girls' and boys' labels from children's clothing, gender neutral uniform is already sweeping through schools.

By Donna Ferguson

For headteacher Jamie Barry, introducing a gender-neutral school uniform policy at his Bristol primary school was just basic common sense. 'Why would we define our children by the clothes they wear? We still have the same uniform, we simply removed all references to gender in our uniform policy.'

Girls at Parson Street school already had the option to wear whatever the boys could wear, but Barry's new policy enabled boys to wear skirts and dresses for the first time. The fact that not a single boy has chosen to do so in the year since the policy was introduced doesn't matter to Barry. 'For me, this was about creating a culture of acceptance. Children are not born homophobic or discriminatory, they are exposed to those influences as they grow up. At Parson Street, we believe children should grow up seeing and experiencing equality, before any stigmas are created.'

This month John Lewis announced it was removing 'girls' and 'boys' labels from its children's clothing departments in order to get rid of gender stereotyping and offer more choice. It is the first retailer to do this but it is following a trend set by many schools. They say it is partly about liberating girls from flimsy shoes, constricting skirts and gender stereotyping but it is also about making all children feel they don't have to be pigeonholed.

Cavendish Road primary in west Didsbury introduced its new policy last September. 'We felt that in this day and age it was inappropriate to designate certain clothing items to one gender,' says the headteacher, Janet Marland.

'We wanted our boys and girls to know they had the same rights. Plus, we had concerns about what some of our girls were wearing – footwear without proper grips or sturdy soles, and tight-fitting pencil skirts that restricted their movement. This was preventing them from playing safely on climbing frames.'

Her policy now simply lists a range of uniform items that parents can choose from when buying for a child of either sex. The removal of references to boys' and girls' clothing was not difficult to do, she says. 'There was no adverse reaction from parents or governors at all. I think all schools can and should have gender-neutral uniform policies.'

Nearly half of women (48%) and more than a third of men (36%) would strongly support schools adopting a gender-neutral uniform policy that allows both boys and girls to wear trousers and skirts, according to a YouGov survey of more than 3,400 UK adults this month. School policies that allow students of either sex to wear trousers but allow only girls – and not boys – to wear skirts, were less popular: only 32% of female and 33% of male respondents supported this approach above others.

Uniform policies that deny pupils any choices are the least popular: just one in 20 women and one in ten men were in favour of policies that force girls to wear skirts and boys to wear trousers. Only 8% of male and 7% of female respondents wanted schools to get rid of skirts so that all children wear trousers.

This is, however, what headteacher Tony Smith has done at Priory school, a comprehensive secondary school in Lewes, East Sussex. 'We often started the school day with conversations about the inappropriate way that young ladies were wearing torn tights and skirts rolled up very high, and the inappropriate way that boys were carrying

off their uniform, with untidy shirts and blazers not worn correctly.' New students of either sex are now only allowed to wear trousers, a shirt and a school jumper, although both girls and boys can also wear PE 'skorts' – skirts with shorts underneath – or PE shorts if there is a heatwave. 'It is a uniform that is smart, practical, cost-effective and decent, and it is the same for everybody.'

While some parents have responded by expressing a desire for their daughter to continue to wear a skirt, many agree with his decision, he says. 'What we're saying is: education is a particular event. Dress appropriately and decently, and come to school to learn. There are plenty of opportunities for you to express your individualism outside school.'

Janet Daulby is a consultant at the Driver Youth Trust charity and campaigns on Twitter against gender stereotyping. She is concerned that girls are often scrutinised far more than boys. 'Boys have got fewer rules to break than girls because there are no sexual messages about boys' uniforms. There are never any stipulations about how short a boy's shorts can be. But if we create rules about skirt lengths, those rules then exist to be broken by girls.'

Schools send a terrible message to boys if they suggest girls should dress modestly to save male staff or students from becoming aroused, she says. 'I think that condones a blame culture for girls and what they wear.'

She and Cheryl Rickman, an ambassador for Let Clothes Be Clothes – which worked with John Lewis to remove its gender labels – are not in favour of forcing girls to wear only what boys were already wearing. 'We need to stop girls feeling like they're wearing a boy's uniform because they wear trousers, which are more practical,' says Rickman. She dislikes the motifs of sequins, hearts and flowers that are frequently found on designated girls' school clothes and shoes because they perpetuate gender stereotypes, and is concerned that girls' school trousers are often tighter fitting than boys'. 'It's important to offer children a choice and recognise that each child is an individual. We want genderless clothing, not genderless children.'

For some schools, though, dividing up girls and boys through uniform is part of their tradition, says Neil Roskilly, chief executive of the Independent Schools Association.

'Each school will make sure their uniform is in line with their values. Parents who don't like that uniform can either choose to take their child to another school or ask the school to review its policy – which I think most would be happy to do.'

Pupils can, of course, make sure their voices are heard. Earlier this year, boys at Isca academy in Devon were denied the right to wear shorts during a heatwave and donned skirts in protest. By the end of the week, headteacher Aimee Mitchell announced that all boys would be allowed to wear shorts next summer, while those who wore skirts would not be punished.

Over in Bristol, Barry is reaping the rewards of his gender-neutral uniform policy. The school recently won a Gold Best Practice award from the LGBT education charity Educate & Celebrate.

'Removing the association of 'boys' or 'girls' with particular clothes in a school uniform policy may not change the way students dress but it could be a huge deal to young people who don't identify as a boy or a girl," he says. "It may give them the acceptance that they need. Until we do that, it's going to be much more difficult for children to say: I am who I am.'

19 September 2017

Gender pay gap in the UK: 2019

An extract from the latest Office for National Statistics statistical bulletin.

Main points

- The gender pay gap among full-time employees stands at 8.9%, little changed from 2018, and a decline of only 0.6 percentage points since 2012.
- The gender pay gap among all employees fell from 17.8% in 2018 to 17.3% in 2019, and continues to decline.
- For age groups under 40 years, the gender pay gap for full-time employees is now close to zero.
- Among 40- to 49-year-olds the gap (currently 11.4%) has decreased substantially over time.
- Among 50- to 59-year-olds and those over 60 years, the gender pay gap is over 15% and is not declining strongly over time.
- One of the reasons for differences in the gender pay gap between age groups is that women over 40 years are more likely to work in lower-paid occupations and, compared with younger women, are less likely to work as managers, directors or senior officials.

The gender pay gap reported by ONS is a long time-series, calculated from the Annual Survey of Hours and Earnings (ASHE) which samples from all employee jobs in all sizes of company. This is different from the gender pay gap based on compulsory reporting for companies with 250 or more employees.

The gender pay gap has been declining slowly in recent years. Among full-time employees it now stands at 8.9%, little changed from 2018 when it was 8.6% (not a statistically significant increase). The figure for 2019 represents a decline of 3.3 percentage points from a decade ago – 12.2% in 2009 – but only 0.6 percentage points since 2012. Among all employees the gap fell from 17.8% in 2018 to 17.3% in 2019.

The gender pay gap is higher for all employees than for each of full-time employees and part-time employees.

This is because women fill more part-time jobs, which have lower hourly median pay than full-time jobs, and are more likely to be in lower-paid occupations.

The gender pay gap is calculated as the difference between average hourly earnings (excluding overtime) of men and women as a proportion of average hourly earnings (excluding overtime) of men's earnings. It is a measure across all jobs in the UK, not of the difference in pay between men and women for doing the same job.

The gender pay gap among full-time employees was 8.9% in 2019

Gender pay gap for median gross hourly earnings (excluding overtime), UK, April 1997 to 2019

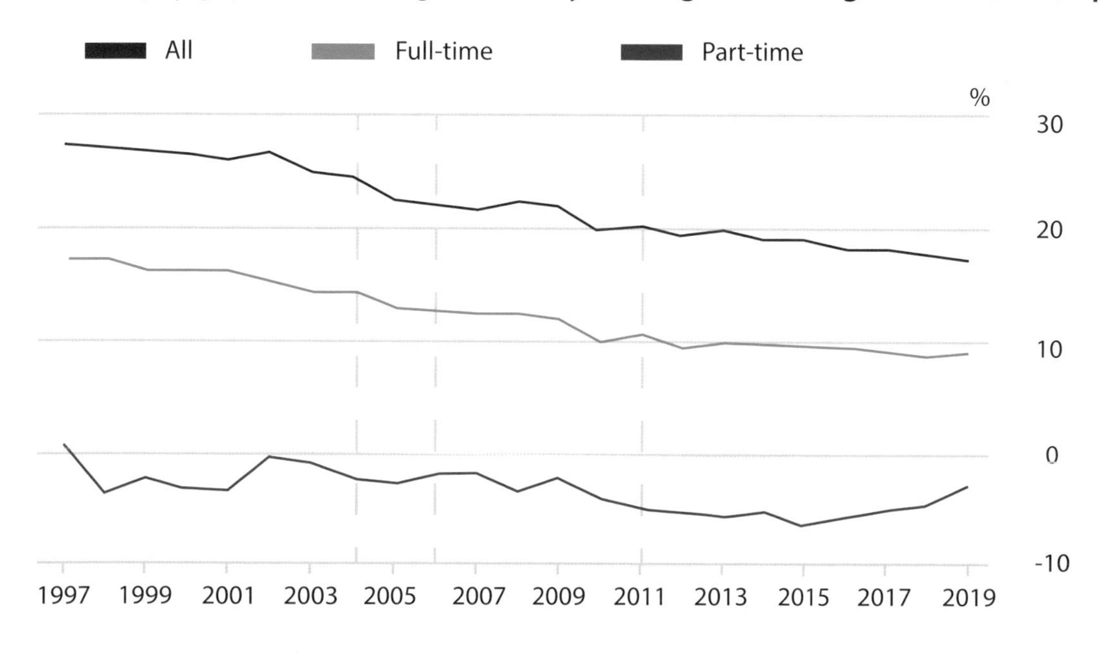

Source: Office for National Statistics - Annual Survey of Hours and Earnings (ASHE)

Notes:

Dashed lines represent discontinuities in 2004, 2006 and 2011 ASHE

The gender pay gap among full-time employees fell in seven of the nine main occupation groups.

Gender pay gap for median gross hourly earnings (excluding overtime) for full-time employees by occupation group, percentage point change, year ending April 2019.

Occupation	Hourly earnings (£)	Gender pay gap	Change from 2018
Managers, directors and senior officials	22.07	15.9	2.0
Professional occupations	21.11	10.1	-1.6
Associate professional and technical occupations	16.28	11.0	-0.9
Skilled trades occupations	12.79	22.4	-1.8
Administrative and secretarial occupations	12.03	4.9	-1.6
Process, plant and machine operatives	11.22	18.1	-0.8
Sales and customer service occupations	10.07	4.4	-0.3
Caring, leisure and other service occupations	10.00	8.0	0.1
Elementary occupations	9.53	11.0	-0.2

Although the estimated gender pay gap among full-time employees in 2019 was no lower than in 2018 (the estimate was 8.9% compared with 8.6% in 2018), it declined in seven of the nine main occupation groupings.

This is one example of the complex nature and interaction of multiple factors that influence the gender pay gap.

An increase in the gender pay gap among the high-paying managers, professionals and senior officials occupation group (from 13.9% to 15.9%) had an effect on the gap, but so too did certain other changes in full-time employment profiles from 2018 to 2019:

- The proportion of employees who held full-time jobs rather than part-time jobs increased more for women than men, but new entrants or returners to full-time jobs are likely to start from a lower pay level and may reduce average pay for full-time women employees.
- The three occupations that saw the largest increase in the proportion of full-time employee jobs held by women were: sales and customer service, elementary occupations and process, and plant and machine operatives; these all have a lower than average rate of hourly pay and will reduce the average full-time earnings among women.

When looking at more specific occupation types, in 2019 there was a gender pay gap of greater than zero in:

- 79% of occupations based on all employees
- 81% based on full-time employees
- 43% based on part-time employees.

The largest gender pay gap among all employees is in carpenters and joiners (44%) and energy plant operatives (41%). The lowest is in archivists and curators (negative 36%), and personal assistants and other secretaries (negative 25%).

29 October 2019

Why Samira Ahmed deserves compensation

The* Newswatch *host's case is not just about gender equality. It questions what value the BBC places on journalism, says her predecessor Raymond Snoddy.

By Raymond Snoddy

As a committed supporter of equal pay for equivalent work at the BBC or anywhere else, it is embarrassing to inadvertently be a possible barrier to Samira Ahmed winning lots of back pay from the corporation.

Ahmed, who has been presenter of the BBC's accountability programme *Newswatch* for the past seven years, is involved in a high-profile equal pay case based on the fact that Jeremy Vine received nearly seven times more than her for presenting *Points Of View*.

Both programmes last 15 minutes and are designed to highlight the opinions of viewers.

The allegation is that the BBC is guilty of gender discrimination – that Vine, the man, received £3,000 a programme and Ahmed, the woman, only £440.

There is one problem. As founding presenter of *Newswatch*, which takes up viewer complaints about BBC television news, I was also paid £440 a programme.

When she took over in 2012, Ahmed, a distinguished BBC journalist, was paid exactly the same, although the fee did rise modestly in subsequent years.

At the superficial level, it must therefore be difficult to argue this is just obvious gender discrimination. A subsidiary argument that women have to spend more time in make-up and therefore should receive more, hardly changes that.

Scratch the surface, however, and there is another equally fundamental issue – how serious journalism is valued compared with 'entertainment'.

> *"Is the BBC saying that a serious trained journalist of either sex doing a difficult job is worth six or seven times less than someone who can sprinkle a little entertainment over their profile?"*

It is the BBC's case that *Points Of View* is a lighthearted entertainment programme that requires a prominent presenter to be 'the audience's friend'. *Newswatch*, which is commissioned by the BBC News channel, is in contrast, a 'serious programme' that needs a trained, serious news journalist, not a presenter with broad audience appeal.

Ahmed has described presenting *Newswatch* as difficult and challenging. She is right. Getting BBC executives to admit that anything the BBC ever does is less than perfect – or even turn up to engage with viewers – is indeed tough.

After interviewing one, now former, senior BBC news executive, my *Newswatch* editor was told it might be a good idea to find a new presenter because the questioning had been too aggressive.

So, let's get this straight. Is the BBC saying that a serious trained journalist of either sex doing a difficult job is worth six or seven times less than someone who can sprinkle a little entertainment over their profile?

In fact, Vine has been a serious journalist for much of his career and can only lay claim to the entertainment mantle, and the greater visibility that goes with it, largely because he appeared on *Strictly Come Dancing*. Ahmed's only mistake may have been not going for dancing lessons.

Seriously, Vine has also been on more prominent programmes for many years than Ahmed and, as a result, has accumulated a greater public persona. Yet there is also a hangover from the past that does discriminate against women. For many years, men were near automatic candidates for top broadcasting jobs. When they move on, agents can go to work on increasing already high salaries.

That is changing, but not quickly enough to help Samira Ahmed. She may not be entitled to the £693,245 she is seeking but the gap between £3,000 and £440 separating two qualified professionals is too great and the employment tribunal should award her compensation.

If she succeeds, it would have serious implications for how the BBC values on-screen journalists compared with entertainers in future.

The BBC insists this case has nothing to do with gender. Does this mean that I too have been seriously underpaid for my eight years as a serious, trained news journalist presenting a serious programme – *Newswatch*?

Time to call the lawyers? Very tempting, but probably not.

1 November 2019

Raymond Snoddy presented *Newswatch* prior to Samira Ahmed.

International Men's Day 2018: the shocking statistics you need to know

By Jack Rear

On Monday 19 November, over 70 countries around the world will celebrate International Men's Day, an annual rallying cry aiming to draw attention to some of the most important issues facing men in the 21st century.

This year, the theme of the event is Positive Male Role Models and companies and public sector organisations across the country, and indeed the world, will be joining together to help bring attention to examples of positive influences for men, particularly with regards to International Men's Day's six pillars: male role models, the positive contribution of men in society, men's health, improving gender relations, highlighting discrimination against men and creating a safer world.

We often hear about the crisis in mental health among men, but that's far from the only field where modern men are struggling. Here are just a few of the shocking statistics around male life in 2018.

On average, 12 men in the British Isles take their lives every single day

Mental health in men is an area which is finally gaining the recognition and attention it deserves after a series of high-profile campaigns from governments, businesses and spokespeople. And there's some evidence to show that we're starting to see some results, particularly in young men.

According to the Samaritans' annual suicide statistics report, the rate of suicides among men in the UK and Ireland under the age of 44 dropped between 2016 and 2017 and the number of male suicides has also been decreasing year on year.

However, there's still a way to go. In 2017, 4,382 men took their own lives, an average of 12 per day. In comparison, 1,439 women died by suicide in the same time frame: about four per day.

Mental health issues in men also disproportionately affect minorities. According to the Lambeth Collective's Black Health and Wellbeing Commission, black men are 17 times more likely to be diagnosed with serious mental health issues. In 2013, the Gay Men's Health Survey found 3% of gay men and 5% of bisexual men attempted suicide that year, compared to 0.4% of heterosexual men.

One in five men die before they hit 65

It's not just mental health where men are in need of intervention. Physical health is also an important talking point for International Men's Day.

According to a report compiled by Men's Health Forum in 2014 and revised in 2017, 19% of men die before their 65th birthday. The biggest cause of death in men is cancer, followed by circulatory diseases.

Men are 14% more likely to get cancer than women and they're 37% more likely to die from the disease. The most common type of cancer in men is prostate cancer which accounts for 25% of all male cancer cases and 13% of deaths from cancer. A quarter of black men will get prostate cancer at some point in their lives.

Part of the problem is that men are less likely to acknowledge illness and don't know as much about their health. Men between the ages of 20 and 40 are half as likely to go to the doctor than women in the same age bracket. Men were also less likely to know about their health status, be able to spot cancer warning signs, and read about medication before taking it.

Men also smoke and drink more than women.

Fewer boys finish secondary education with a minimum of five C grades at GCSE, including English and Maths

Education is another area where boys are falling behind girls. Girls are 20% more likely to finish secondary school with five C grades or higher at GCSE, according to the Department for Education's statistics.

In addition, boys are less likely to be high achievers in school. The stats show that 52.5% of boys achieve a minimum of five A*– C grades at GCSE compared to 61.8% of girls.

A 2014 report also showed that boys are three times more likely than girls to be excluded or expelled from school.

The educational attainment gap begins at school but continues to echo through men's lives. According to data from UCAS, in 2017 over 71,000 less men were accepted to UK universities than women. In the class of 2017, men make up around 43% of new freshers.

In apprenticeships too, there's a gender gap. According to government data in the 2016/17 intake cycle, young men made up only 46% of total hires.

And while we often hear that professions such as medicine and law are dominated by men, that may not be the case for much longer. Data from the General Medical Council shows that year on year fewer men are entering high skill professions such as dentistry, medicine, law and education.

As it stands, the Department for Education does not fund any initiatives aimed at addressing the underachievement of boys in education.

There are also a significant lack of male role models in schools. In England, just 26.2%pc of teachers (15.2% in primary schools), 8.5% of teaching assistants, and 18% of support staff are men.

Men are twice as likely to be a victim of violent crime

That's according to a 2013 report from the Office for National Statistics, which found that trend also holds true in children. Men also make up around 78% of the perpetrators of violent crime, according to the ONS.

A 2009 policing report found that around two-thirds of murder victims are men.

While women are significantly more likely to suffer domestic abuse than men, that's not to say that men aren't also victimised in their own homes. Just over 13% of men say they've been a victim of domestic abuse at some point in their lives. In fact, in every three reports of domestic abuse, one victim is male.

Again, this is significantly more of a problem in the gay community. In 2008/09 6.2% of gay and bisexual men said they'd suffered domestic abuse, compared to 3.3% of heterosexual men.

But men are also significantly less likely to tell anyone if they've suffered domestic abuse. 10pc will tell the police (compared to 26% of women), 11pc will tell a health professional (compared to 23% of women) and 23% will tell someone else in a position of authority (compared to 46% of women).

There is also a significant dearth of support for men suffering from domestic abuse. In the UK there are a total of 93 spaces offering refuge or safe houses for male victims of domestic violence, and only 22 of these are male only. For women, there are around 4,000 of these refuges. There is no refuge for men in London.

Around 1,000 men are raped every month

In a year when high-profile male victims of sexual harassment, such as Terry Crews and Anthony Rapp, have come forward about their experiences, it's also worth shining a light on the fact that it isn't just women who suffer from sexual violence. According to a 2017 crime survey by the ONS, in 2017 alone there were around 138,000 reports of sexual assaults against men that year. It's also likely this could be an underestimation due to men not coming forward about their assaults. The charity Rape Crisis found

that every year, an average of around 1,000 men are raped every month in England and Wales alone.

This is a particular problem in the gay community. According to a survey from the Gay Men's Health Project 62% of gay men have been groped without consent, and 30% described themselves as a 'survivor of sexual assault, abuse or rape.'

In addition, according to the Government's revenge porn helpline, around a quarter of victims of revenge porn (the sharing of explicit photos and images by an ex or current partner) are men.

One in every five victims of forced marriage is a man, according to a report from ONS statistics.

Around one million children in the UK have no contact with their fathers

According to the ONS there are about 2.8 million lone-parent families. Of these families, the percentage being headed by men has stayed at around 10% over the past decade according to Gingerbread, a resource centre for single-parent families. The Centre for Social Justice estimated that around one million children in the UK are living with no contact with their father at all. A 2008 report found that the vast majority of single parents don't receive child support payments.

But that's not to say that some fathers aren't trying. The Nuffield Foundation reported in 2015 that 96% of parents fighting in court for access to their children are fathers.

86% of rough sleepers are men

Homelessness is an issue which disproportionately affects men. A 2017 study from the Ministry of Housing, Communities and Social Affairs found that 86% of rough sleepers are men.

Homeless charity Crisis also reports that 84% of hidden homeless people (people who are at risk of eviction, sofa-surfing at friends and family, or living in unsatisfactory conditions) are men.

Figures compiled earlier this year found that between 2013 and 2017 the amount of homeless people who've died on the streets or in temporary accommodation has doubled and around 90% of those deaths were men.

19 November 2018

www.telegraph.co.uk

Formula 1: there can be no equality in sport while women's bodies are used for promotions

***An article from* The Conversation.**

THE CONVERSATION

By Anna Tippett

The Dutch politician Roy van Aalst has spoken out against the removal of grid girls from Formula 1 motor racing, arguing that it is a way of patronising women. He boasted that the right-wing nationalist political party to which he belongs, Party for Freedom (PVV), will ensure that the grid girls are reinstated at the Zandvoort grand prix in 2020.

> *"Only a huge idiot can see a beautiful woman as a problem,' he said. 'The rest of the people love it. It is part of motorsport and the PVV wants us to ensure that next year this beautiful tradition will be restored to its former glory."*

The replacement of grid girls with grid kids in 2018 marked a shift in Formula 1 to a more family-friendly atmosphere. But van Aalst's comments echo the backlash against this transition – which included some grid girls arguing that they were being denied the right to work by 'feminists'. Grid girl Lauren-Jade Pope took to Twitter to object:

> *"Get me on @thismorning so I can defend us #gridgirls. These feminists have cost us our jobs! I have been a grid girl for 8 years and I have never felt uncomfortable! I love my job, if I didn't I wouldn't do it! No-one forces us to do this! This is our choice!"*
>
> ***– Lauren-Jade (@laurenjadepope) January 31, 2018***

Remarkably, the 'feminists' so often mentioned in the debate were actually the Formula 1 bosses themselves. They made the decision to stop using grid girls because they no longer resonated with their brand values – with Sean Bratches, the managing director of commercial operations at Formula 1, stating that the inclusion of grid girls was 'at odds with modern-day societal norms'.

Employment opportunity?

One of the main criticisms of the scrapping of grid girls was that women would be out of work. Such criticism drew attention to the earnings that would be lost by the women as well as the idea that the decision was denying them their 'right to choose' to use their bodies for aesthetic purposes and financial gain. The role of the grid girls was to carry out promotional tasks, most of which included bearing the names of sponsors to the public and cheering on the all-male racing drivers.

Prominent figures, including World Champion Lewis Hamilton, have called for the return of the grid girls. Hamilton's rationale that 'women are the most beautiful thing in the world', alongside Ferrari driver Sebastian Vettel stating he 'likes women' because 'they look beautiful', serve to emphasise the deep-rooted sexism still entrenched in the motor sporting world. There is still a long way to go to eliminate these outdated views, particularly in sports such as motor racing which are traditionally categorised as male.

Testimonials from former grid girls have indicated that their earnings were around £300 per day, bearing in mind the work was intermittent. Household names such as Kelly Brook, Melinda Messenger and Jodie Marsh all began their 'careers' as grid girls, later crossing over to glamour modelling in lads' mags and the like.

During the backlash to the decision in 2018, grid girl testimonies sought to label feminists as bigoted, with headlines 'hitting back' at 'middle-class feminists who are forcing other women out of work'.

No equality, no empowerment

Unequal representation in Formula 1 promotional modelling was itself enough to refute arguments of unfair treatment regarding employment being lost. The lack of promotional models from BME groups alongside the complete omission of men from this role highlighted a clear lack of equal opportunity (if you can call sexual objectification that). Promotional modelling also carries a rigid time limit, with 'careers' in this field usually having to end by women's mid-to-late 20s.

The message sent, particularly to young girls, was that motor racing is a male sport and – if you're keen to be involved in it – you should aspire to be beautiful, sexualise yourself, and be prepared to drape yourself over cars and male racing drivers like an accessory.

This is a stark departure from the message being sent today, where excited grid kids – male and female – now walk on the grid with ambitions of becoming racing drivers themselves. Formula 1 must hold onto this message and not revert back to one that degrades, demoralises and dehumanises its female supporters.

That said, although Formula 1 has made progress, promotional modelling is still a feature across other sporting events, including walk-on girls (darts and cycling), ring girls (wrestling and boxing) and cheerleaders (football and basketball). Although darts walkon girls were also axed in 2018, they made a recent 'one off' return at the German Darts Grand Prix, supposedly due to prior sponsorship agreements.

There are also the 'Crystals', the all-female cheerleaders of Crystal Palace FC, who appear wearing bikinis in a promotional video for the club. Not so inspiring for any budding female footballers.

Full speed ahead

Formula 1's move away from grid girls has indeed made it a more inclusive sport and it is time for other industries to follow its lead. Until women are given equal opportunities in sport, they will continue to be underpaid, undervalued and underrated.

Roy van Aalst's assumption that only 'huge idiots' can find beautiful women a problem emphasises the crude ignorance inherent in the many debates over the sexualisation of popular culture. Of course 'beautiful women' are not a problem – nor are beautiful men, or beautiful people in general. But when you display only one sex as 'beautiful' – although I think 'sexualised' would be a more fitting word for the grid girls – you serve to diminish half of society.

They are to be gazed upon and are never themselves given the authority to be the 'gazers'. This is how you alienate women from aspiring to be sporting champions and instead relegate them to the sidelines, encouraging them to only ever be the cheerleaders.

If upholding the stance that favours gender equality makes me a 'huge idiot', then I am confidently and proudly one. I'm sure my daughter will thank me for it.

24 June 2019

Gender equality is not a 'women's issue' – it's good for men too

There are plenty of proud male feminists, but to make equality a reality we need to draw more into the conversation.

By Julia Gillard

Men have always played critical roles in the women's movement. From John Stuart Mill to Fredrick Douglass, male allies have long supported the struggle for gender equality. And today there are plenty of men who are proud feminists – just ask Andy Murray, who hired and championed a female coach, Amélie Mauresmo; or Ryan Gosling, who has become something of a feminist icon. But there is still a long way to go, and we'll only get there by drawing more men into the conversation.

Despite all the progress made, men still dominate positions of power. And, as a string of recent harassment scandals has shown, the behaviour of some men has had profound effects on women's careers, their success and their lives. The good news, as we mark International Women's Day, is that many men are acknowledging the importance of playing their part to make gender equality a reality.

A new study by Ipsos Mori, in collaboration with the Global Institute for Women's Leadership at King's College London (of which I am the chair) and International Women's Day, has found that while a third of British men think they are being expected to do too much to support women's equality, far more – half – do not. In fact, three in five men in Britain agree that gender equality won't be achieved unless they also take action to support women's rights.

Despite attempts in some quarters to paint gender equality as a zero-sum game, there are plenty of win-win propositions for these men to advocate. Better parental leave for fathers would be a good start. Sorry, Piers Morgan, but the vast majority of respondents to our survey don't believe that childcare is emasculating, with 75% of people globally disagreeing that a man who stays at home to look after his children is less of a man.

Government policy needs to catch up with this new reality, and the evidence is clear that, unless paternity leave is non-transferable and well paid, uptake will be low. Sweden and Norway show us that the introduction of the 'daddy quota' – the period of parental leave reserved specifically for fathers – has a positive effect on male take-up of parental leave, and then on men's long-term involvement in household work and childcare. This reaps economic dividends, as women's talents are no longer lost to the labour force, and having an involved father has a positive effect on children's wellbeing.

Men want employers to do more. Globally, three-quarters (72%) agree that employers should make it easier for men to combine childcare with work. We are seeing an increasing number of jobs that offer flexible working schemes to do just this, but too often they are targeted at women, and associated with being on the 'mummy track'. We need to tackle this flexibility stigma, and the most effective way to do so would be to encourage more men to take on part-time and flexible work.

Businesses need not fear: research links flexible working to increased productivity, as better work-life balance leads to happier, more effective workers.

Women gain from having flexible partners, too. A study of German couples found that having a partner who works flexibly boosted the wages of men and women, with the effect most pronounced for mothers. Conversely, women whose partners work very long hours are significantly more likely to quit the labour force – taking their talent and experience with them.

For those who wonder why, on International Women's Day, I'm writing an article focusing on men, I hope you've detected something of a theme. Gender equality is not a 'women's issue'. As the theme for IWD this year encapsulates, it is better for balance, better for all of us.

8 March 2019

- Julia Gillard is a former Australian prime minister and leader of the Labour party from 2010 to 2013. She is chair of the Global Institute for Women's Leadership.

www.theguardian.com

Actions matter more than words when parents are helping children understand gender equality

What parents do, as well as what they say matters a great deal when it comes to children forming opinions about gender roles later on in life, says new research which uses longitudinal data from Understanding Society and its predecessor the British Household Panel Survey (BHPS).

The research published in the *European Sociological Review* discovered whether saying or doing makes more of an impact when it comes to shaping children's attitudes to gender roles. For example, if a child saw their father doing the housework at home, are they more likely to form a better attitude towards gender equality later in adulthood?

The team from the London School of Economics used data from Understanding Society and its predecessor, the British Household Panel Survey and focused on British children aged between 11 and 15. All Understanding Society participants aged 10-15 fill in a multitopic paper questionnaire every year.

The main sample comprised of 2,859 children (1,387 girls and 1,472 boys) who were both living in couple-parent families. However, for completeness, the study also repeated the analysis with 897 young people living in lone-mother families since single-parent (overwhelmingly lone-mother) families are likely to have a rather different influence on their children's attitudes in the absence of a father.

Key findings

- Seeing a mother as a housewife is a strong predictor of children believing in gender inequality later on in life – this mattered more than either mothers' or fathers' own attitudes.
- Having a mother in full-time work is associated with less traditional attitudes.
- Boys are more affected by their fathers than by their mothers: fathers' traditionalism influences boys even if mothers are not traditional, while mothers' traditionalism only influences boys if fathers are also traditional.
- Girls are influenced by the traditionalism of both parents.
- In lone-mother households, mothers' attitudes did not provide a greater influence on sons, but mothers' share of time as a housewife continued to be influential.
- Seeing parental behaviours are more influential than parental attitudes when children are developing their own attitudes towards gender equality.

Why was longitudinal data needed for this study?

Professor Lucinda Platt from the London School of Economics said, 'We confirmed that attitudes formed in childhood, summarised using prospective measures that are not confounded by adaptation to partnership or labour market context, do persist into adult life and have measurable consequences for behaviours. We have thus shown how intergenerational transmission of spoken and enacted gender roles has the potential to impact gender relations in adults' lives and is likely to be part of the cause of persistent inequalities in paid and unpaid work. Following sons and daughters further into adulthood and identifying the pathways for both the retention and adaptation of gender-role attitudes will be a valuable future extension of these findings.'

9 January 2017

Platt, L. and Polavieja, J. (2016). 'Saying and Doing Gender: Intergenerational Transmission of Attitudes towards the Sexual Division of Labour.' European Sociological Review, 32 (6): 820-834. doi:10.1093/esr/jcw037.

Understanding Society is an initiative funded by the Economic and Social Research Council and various Government Departments, with scientific leadership by the Institute for Social and Economic Research, University of Essex, and survey delivery by NatCen Social Research and Kantar Public. The research data are distributed by the UK Data Service.

'Pink tax' on perfume: Women are being charged more for female fragrances than men are for aftershave

Female consumers pay on average 60p more per 10ml of fragrance than men do on the aftershave equivalents.

By Katie Grant

UK shoppers are paying nearly £14 more on average for a Dolce & Gabbana perfume for women than on the male aftershave equivalent, according to the research. Women in the UK are being charged more for big name perfumes than men are for the male aftershave equivalent in the latest example of the so-called Pink Tax in action, research indicates.

Female consumers pay on average 60 pence more per 10ml of fragrance than male shoppers, suggesting the existence of a Pink Tax on perfume, according to data published by a price comparison site.

What is the pink tax?

The term 'pink tax' refers to the extra money women are charged for certain products or services above the standard cost for comparable goods aimed at men; often these items are coloured pink to indicate they have been developed for female consumers.

Last month some shoppers accused Gillette of hypocrisy when the firm released an advert aimed at tackling 'toxic masculinity', arguing the shaving brand charges more for women's razors than for men's ones.

Now, ahead of Valentine's Day – one of the biggest shopping events of the year for the fragrance industry – it has emerged that UK customers will typically pay six pence more per millilitre for scents marketed at women than for those aimed at men.

In January this year the average price of a 100ml bottle of Burberry Brit For Her eau de toilette cost £24.90, while the same sized bottle of Burberry Brit for Men eau de toilette typically retailed at £23.69, data from Idealo shows.

Eau de Rip Off

UK shoppers paid £64.09 on average for 200ml Dolce & Gabbana Light Blue eau de toilette for women, nearly £14 more than they were charged for the brand's Light Blue Pour Homme equivalent, which typically sold for £50.65.

And 50ml of Carolina Herrera CH for women eau de toilette cost £40.81, compared to £36.59 for the men's fragrance.

There was no difference in price for some perfumes and aftershaves – both the male and female versions of Diesel's Zero Plus eau de toilette retailed at £12.54, according to Idealo.

In some cases men's scents were more expensive – Roberto Cavalli's Just Cavalli Man eau de toilette (50ml) typically retailed at £11.37, while the brand's Just Cavalli Woman cost £10.97.

But where there were price discrepancies the figures show that the vast majority of fragrances aimed at women cost more than the male aftershave equivalents.

Cheaper prices for men

Katy Phillips, an Idealo spokeswoman, suggested some women may attempt to circumvent this surcharge by choosing to wear fragrances aimed at men instead of the female options.

'It wouldn't be the first time that women have played brands at their own game by ditching the 'pink' or women's version of a product in order to take advantage of the cheaper prices enjoyed by men,' Ms Phillips said.

Some women have reported buying men's razors 'because they are cheaper and better', after Gillette came under scrutiny last month, she added.

12 February 2019

www.inews.co.uk

45 per cent of gamers are women. But in every other way they're still not equal to men

Mirror's Edge Catalyst, Dishonored 2... ***more and more games have females as leads. But the gaming world is still too much of a boy's club.***

By Vanessa Tsai

45% of video gamers, and 46% of game purchasers, are women. More complex storylines, more personalised characters, more acceptance of 'geekiness' as something to be proud of and a wider variety of games available are just a few of the reasons why gaming is no longer being seen as a boys-only club

Women are finding their place in the gaming world

GirlGamerGaB, a YouTuber and gamer with 60,000 subscribers, is excited about the change. 'More and more I feel like it is normal for a woman to play video games too. It's no longer 'a guy thing'. Growing up I often heard 'What, you play video games?! That's so awesome, girls never play video games!', but now when you tell someone you play video games you'd sooner get the question what kind of games you're into, which is really nice.'

And yet, even the fantasy world still isn't equal.

But from gamers, to game developers, to women in games, we still have a long way to go before gaming becomes a gender-equal world.

...for women who play games:

On paper, a female gamer's customer experience should be no different to that of a man's. In practice, the communal nature of gaming means that male gamers can make life pretty unpleasant for a female gamer... a 'side effect' of the product she didn't sign up for.

Women face roughly three times more harassment than men when playing online. Gamer and YouTuber Yasmin Uddin (known as Yammy xox) said she experienced sexism first hand, 'mostly during games like *Call of Duty* and *Gears of War*. I was ashamed to speak in online game chat as I felt as if I'd be ridiculed for my voice.... I'd be told to 'get back into the kitchen.'

It's not always that aggressive – but unwanted attention is still a distraction to women just looking to play the game. 'A lot of people try to make flirty conversation whenever they find out I'm a female gamer, and ask for my personal details, like Facebook or Skype,' says Hayley W, an avid gamer.

And sometimes, men will be unnecessarily forgiving towards a woman – skewing her results in the game. 'They're a lot more forgiving to me if I make mistakes. They assume I'm not as good as them and sometimes give me game money in an attempt to flirt.'

...for women in games:

In a make-believe universe where anything is possible, is it really so hard to picture female characters without pinched waists, hourglass curves, and tiny, tiny skirts? Despite managing to come up with a seemingly endless amount of alternate worlds and fantastical societies, games often fall back on the same old tropes of women wearing clothes which, if you think about it, are highly impractical for the things they're expected to do within the game.

Still, things are improving: a recent survey pointed to a decrease in the sexualisation of female protagonists in games over the last eight years. More and more women are being given three-dimensional roles and complex personalities. Just give them some clothes, too?

...for women in the gaming industry:

Most games are created by men, for men. Governments around the world are talking about the lack of women in STEM (science, tech, engineering, maths) – for the gaming world, the problem manifests itself in fewer female coders and developers to create games.

All programmers and engineers

years experience in the industry

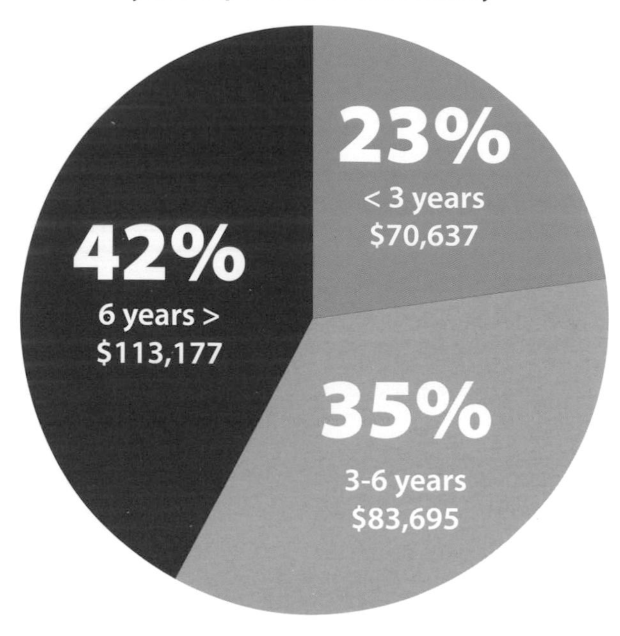

Gender stats %

Gender	Represented	Average salary
Men	95%	$93,977
Women	5%	$79,319

All artists and animators

years experience in the industry

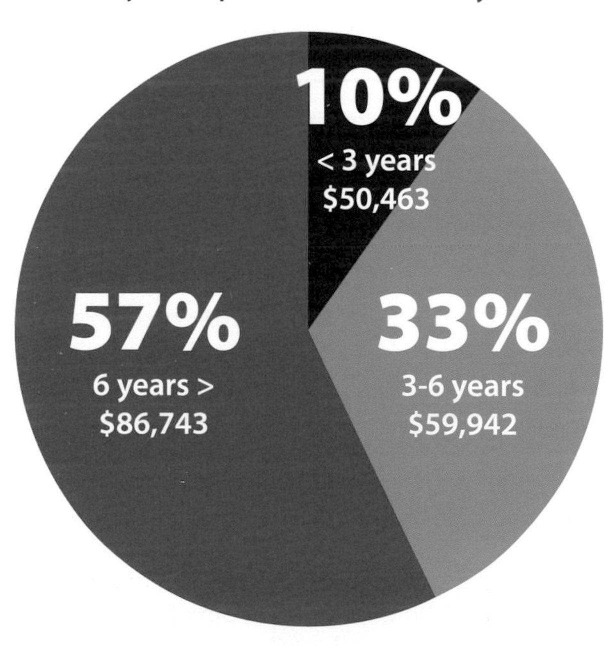

Gender stats %

Gender	Represented	Average salary
Men	91%	$76,054
Women	9%	$55,909

Source: ecnmy.org

Those who do make it into the industry, face lower salaries for doing – you guessed it – exactly the same job – women in gaming in the US, for example, make 86 cents for every dollar made by a man in the industry.

Women working in gaming have also been known to face vicious and sexist abuse from gamers – you need only to look at the #GamerGate controversy, where several women working in the industry faced an orchestrated online campaign of misogynistic harassment and threats, to see that the cost of working in gaming for women is higher than just the pay gap.

...but things are changing:

With the recognition that almost an equal number of women and men are playing video games, the gaming world is slowly realising it's got to change.

After #GamerGate, Intel pledged $300 million towards a programme called 'Diversity in Technology'. Support groups have sprung up across the gaming community, offering a protective network for women working in the industry, promoting diversity in video game development, and encouraging girls to get involved in gaming and STEM.

With more women working behind the scenes in creating games, more diverse women represented in games, and more women playing games and hosting gaming channels, more and more girls are being encouraged to get into gaming. Major studios are no longer afraid to turn away from traditionally male-dominated games to ones starring female leads – *Mirror's Edge Catalyst*, and *Dishonored 2* are just a couple of examples.

Being a female gamer on YouTube has definitely enabled many girls to feel as if they aren't alone, Yasmin says. 'Many of my young audience [she has 90,000 subscribers] comment telling me that they aspire to open a channel like mine and show the world their passion for games, and just knowing that makes me feel incredibly happy!'

Yasmin is part of an ever-growing community of female gamers is making their voices heard – women can play games, they can star in them, and then can even make their own.

7 March 2017

Gender stereotyping

The international human rights law framework prohibits gender stereotypes and stereotyping which undermine the enjoyment of human rights and fundamental freedoms. States have obligation to eliminate discrimination against women and men in all areas of their lives. This obligation requires states to take measures to address gender stereotypes both in public and private life as well as to refrain from stereotyping.

*A **gender stereotype** is a generalised view or preconception about attributes or characteristics, or the roles that are or ought to be possessed by, or performed by women and men. A gender stereotype is harmful when it limits women's and men's capacity to develop their personal abilities, pursue their professional careers and make choices about their lives.*

Harmful stereotypes can be both hostile/negative (e.g. women are irrational) or seemingly benign (e.g. women are nurturing). For example, the fact that childcare responsibilities often fall exclusively on women is based on the latter stereotype.

***Gender stereotyping** refers to the practice of ascribing to an individual woman or man specific attributes, characteristics or roles by reason only of her or his membership in the social group of women or men. Gender stereotyping is wrongful when it results in a violation or violations of human rights and fundamental freedoms.*

Examples of wrongful gender stereotyping are the failure to criminalise marital rape based on societal perception of women as the sexual property of men, and the failure to effectively investigate, prosecute and sentence sexual violence against women based on, e.g. the stereotype that women should protect themselves from sexual violence by dressing and behaving modestly.

Gender stereotypes compounded and intersecting with other stereotypes have a disproportionate negative impact on certain groups of women, such as women from minority or indigenous groups, women with disabilities, women from lower caste groups or with lower economic status, migrant women, etc.

Wrongful gender stereotyping is a frequent cause of discrimination against women and a contributing factor in violations of a vast array of rights such as the right to health, adequate standard of living, education, marriage and family relations, work, freedom of expression, freedom of movement, political participation and representation, effective remedy, and freedom from gender-based violence.

Fawcett research shows exposure to gender stereotypes as a child causes harm in later life

The Fawcett Society is today publishing new research which highlights the lifelong impact of gender stereotyping in childhood. In new polling, 45% of people said that when they were children, they experienced gender stereotyping as they were expected to behave in a certain way. Stereotyping in childhood has wide-ranging and significant negative consequences for both women and men, with more than half (51%) of people affected saying it constrained their career choices and 44% saying it harmed their personal relationships.

Half of all women affected (53%) said gender stereotyping had a negative impact on who does the caring in their own family. Older women were particularly affected by this. Seven in ten younger women (18–34s) affected by stereotypes say their career choices were restricted.

Boys and men feel it too. 69% of men aged under 35 said that gender stereotyping of children has a damaging effect on perceptions of what it means to be a man or a woman.

Men were as likely as women to say that gender stereotypes they experienced had negatively affected their relationships.

Sam Smethers, Fawcett Society Chief Executive, said:

"Gender stereotypes hold us all back. We have boys who cannot express their emotions, become aggressive, under-achieve at school and go on to be part of a culture of toxic masculinity which normalises violence. We have girls who have low self-esteem and issues with their body image, with one in five 14-year-old girls self-harming. We have a heavily segregated labour market where just 8% of STEM apprentices are women. Gender stereotyping is at the root of all of this. We have to grasp the challenge to change it."

The new data comes as the Fawcett Society publishes a review of evidence showing that harmful stereotypes are not only endemic, but they are unwittingly and repeatedly replicated and taught across society. Parents with new babies and young children inadvertently reinforce gender

stereotypes creating a 'gendered world' through toys, play, language and environment. Teachers differently reward boys' and girls' behaviour, and representations in children's stories are often stereotyped. By age two children are aware of gender and, as early as six years old, children associate intelligence with being male, and 'niceness' with being female.

The report points to the damaging impact this has, drawing links between gender stereotypes held by adolescents and violence against women and girls, and the direct impact on the gender pay gap of the low take-up amongst young women of science, technology and maths subjects. Amid a crisis of self-harm among young women in particular, the report cites evidence that children whose friendship groups emphasise traditional gender stereotypes have lower wellbeing.

Sam Smethers added:

"This isn't a trivial issue about who wears pink or blue, gender stereotypes are harmful. But the evidence is clear, the wiring in our brains is soft not hard. We can challenge attitudes and change lives, but we must wake up to the harm that gender stereotypes are doing to all of us and the price that we are paying for it."

The research also identifies key interventions, particularly aimed at younger children, which work to challenge and change gender norms and mitigate against the harms seen in later life.

- children's literature that challenges gender norms can undo children's previously held perceptions
- whole-school approaches to gender stereotyping have demonstrated positive results
- In Sweden challenging gender stereotypes is an explicit requirement of the school curriculum.

Additional key findings

- a majority of under 35s agree that stereotypes have wide-ranging adverse effects on children's subject choices at school, young people's career choices, attitudes to who does the caring and attitudes to what it means to be a man or a woman
- 54% of women aged over 35 affected by childhood stereotypes say they negatively affected decisions about whose job it is to care for others in your own family, compared with 38% of men aged over 35.
- 46% of people agree government should take action to challenge gender stereotyping.

The Fawcett Society plans to launch a 'Commission on Gender Stereotypes in Early Childhood' to raise awareness, build a new consensus on the issue and examine the evidence of what works to challenge stereotypes, change childhood and change lives.

7 March 2019

How to beat gender stereotypes: learn, speak up and react

By Ina Toegel, Professor of Leadership and Organisational Change, IMD Business School and Maude Lavanchy, Research Associate, IMD Business School

"Life is not fair; get used to it." The famous first rule of Bill Gates' *11 rules you will never learn in school* resonates with everybody, but probably more with women than men.

According to the *Global Gender Gap Index*, 108 years are needed to close the global gender gap. While classical economic models predict that discrimination on the basis of characteristics such as gender should naturally disappear thanks to competition, reality seems to tell a different story.

The lack of women in male-dominated and high-paying industries such as STEM (science, technology, engineering and mathematics) is often cited as a critical factor behind the gender gap. Even though girls perform as well as boys in math and science standardised tests at school, fewer women consider a professional career in these fields. Women seem to face different hurdles that have little to do with their abilities. Gender stereotypes are one of them.

What are gender stereotypes?

While men are generally portrayed as having agency characteristics such as competence, achievement-orientation, inclination to take charge, autonomy and rationality, women are associated with communal characteristics such as concern for others, affiliation tendencies, deference and emotional sensitivity. These characteristics are not only different, they tend to be oppositional: lay people on average believe that men should not be excessively warm (communal) and that women should not be excessively dominant (agency). Research on these generalisations has been extensive and shows they are consistent across culture, time and context.

Stereotypes often serve as shortcuts for forming impressions of people guide our decisions, without people being completely aware of it. Gender preconceptions have important consequences for the workplace. Here are some examples:

• *No credit where credit is due*

Whenever women are working with men on male gender-typed tasks, men are more likely to be credited for joint successes and women are more likely to be blamed for joint failures. These negative performance expectations can only be overturned when the woman's individual contribution is unquestionable, or her task competence is very high

• *Men are promoted on potential, women are promoted for proven performance*

Research shows that women are held to stricter standards for promotion: promoted women have higher performance ratings than promoted men, and performance ratings are more strongly related to promotions for women than for men.

• *The backlash effect: competent but bossy and unlikeable*

When women counter their stereotype and break expectations about how they 'should' behave, they pay the cost: dominant women are perceived as less likeable and less hireable than men. A 2016 survey of more than 30,000 employees found that women who negotiated for promotions were 30% more likely than men to be labelled intimidating, bossy or aggressive.

The paradox: defy or conform?

When women conform to gender stereotypes (e.g. by showing emotional sensitivity and concern for others), they are likely to be perceived as less competent. But, if they defy these stereotypes and behave 'like a man' (e.g. by showing dominance, ambition and rationality), they will be penalised by a backlash effect. Successful women in male gender-typed fields are well aware of this effect. Speaking at the American Economic Association's annual meeting in January, Susan Athey, a world-renowned economist, said:

> *"I spent all my time hoping that no one would remember I was female."*

Men, too, can be penalised when they do not conform to these gender stereotypes. A recent study found that the gender of the initial role occupant (a microcredit loan manager in this case) was enough to influence the authority enjoyed by future individuals in that role. In other words, when a borrower was paired with a female manager, he/she gender-typed the role as a female-typed role and was less compliant than if he/she was initially paired with a male manager. This bias remains even after being subsequently managed by the other gender (i.e. a male manager in our example).

Stereotypes harm us all

Stereotypes are entrenched beliefs perpetuated by both men and women, present in our minds since childhood. Anybody can easily fall into this trap. Curious? You can test your unconscious association between gender and science/arts by taking the Gender-Career Implicit Association Test. 70% of people who took this test across 34 countries associated science as being more male than female.

Unfortunately, anti-discrimination legislation, codes of conduct, diversity criteria or legal actions can't fight this more subtle form of discrimination. You can't sue your boss for consciously or unconsciously believing that you don't have what it takes to succeed.

The ball is in our court

Raising awareness of these challenges alone is insufficient. To change mindsets, women should do three things:

1. Learn – because knowledge is power

Have you ever had the feeling of having been ripped off by your repair shop? If yes, you are not alone. A research paper found that auto-repair shops alter their price quotes depending on how informed callers appear to be about prices. When callers signalled that they had no idea about what the repair should cost, women were quoted a higher price than men. But these gender differences disappeared when a benchmark price was indicated.

This example illustrates how a single piece of information could help reduce any gender-related price discrimination (and might also start changing car mechanics' expectations about women). Interestingly, the study also found that repair shops were more likely to offer a lower price if asked by a woman than by a man. So, informed women ended up having an advantage over men.

The #SheCANics movement is a powerful example of empowering women through awareness, education and support.

2. Move confidently into male-dominated areas and speak up

Let's be honest: stereotypes won't disappear unless people understand they are harmful. Women in male-dominated environments can help raise awareness. Role models play a crucial role in promoting gender equality and fighting gender stereotypes (e.g. Billie Jean King in sport, Sheryl Sandberg's Lean In initiative and the #banbossy campaign). Even advertisers are moving into this space and are starting to actively address women (e.g. Gillette's ad 'The Best Men Can Be' or Serena Williams' Bumble commercial).

3. Prepare to react

Women should anticipate and prepare to react to inappropriate or discriminating comments. For example, when the American celebrity Lauren Conrad was asked on radio 'What is your favorite position?', she briefly paused and replied 'CEO'.

While such questions or comments were acceptable in the past, it is our role today to make sure they will no longer be tolerated. Those perpetuating gender stereotypes should bear the consequences of such behaviour. A recent example is Martin Solveig's apology after making a sexist comment during the Ballon d'Or ceremony. We must accept that biases exist, own them and retrain our brains to overcome them. Life might not be fair, but we can do something about it.

7 March 2019

Ban on harmful gender stereotypes in ads comes into force

CAP's (Committees of Advertising Practice) new rule banning harmful gender stereotypes in ads has come into force.

The new rule in the Advertising Codes, which will apply to broadcast and non-broadcast media (including online and social media), states:

> *"[Advertisements] must not include gender stereotypes that are likely to cause harm, or serious or widespread offence."*

This change follows a review of gender stereotyping in ads by the Advertising Standards Authority (ASA) – the body that administers the UK Advertising Codes. The review found evidence suggesting that harmful stereotypes can restrict the choices, aspirations and opportunities of children, young people and adults and these stereotypes can be reinforced by some advertising, which plays a part in unequal gender outcomes.

Following the review, CAP consulted publicly on specific proposals to ban harmful gender stereotypes in ads, underpinned by the evidence collected by the ASA. The proposed restrictions were supported by a majority of respondents.

The evidence does not show that the use of gender stereotypes is always problematic and the new rule does not seek to ban gender stereotypes outright, but to identify specific harms that should be prevented.

The advertising industry has had six months to get ready for the new rule. The ASA will now deal with any complaints it receives on a case-by-case basis and will assess each ad by looking at the content and context to determine if the new rule has been broken.

Scenarios in ads likely to be problematic under the new rule include:

- An ad that depicts a man with his feet up and family members creating mess around a home while a woman is solely responsible for cleaning up the mess.
- An ad that depicts a man or a woman failing to achieve a task specifically because of their gender, for example a man's inability to change nappies; a woman's inability to park a car.
- Where an ad features a person with a physique that does not match an ideal stereotypically associated with their gender, the ad should not imply that their physique is a significant reason for them not being successful, for example in their romantic or social lives.
- An ad that seeks to emphasise the contrast between a boy's stereotypical personality (e.g. daring) with a girl's stereotypical personality (e.g. caring) needs to be handled with care.
- An ad aimed at new mums which suggests that looking attractive or keeping a home pristine is a priority over other factors such as their emotional wellbeing.
- An ad that belittles a man for carrying out stereotypically 'female' roles or tasks.

The rule and its supporting guidance doesn't stop ads from featuring:

- A woman doing the shopping or a man doing DIY.
- Glamorous, attractive, successful, aspirational or healthy people or lifestyles.
- One gender only, including in ads for products developed for and aimed at one gender.
- Gender stereotypes as a means to challenge their negative effects.

CAP will carry out a review of the new rule in 12 months' time to make sure it's meeting its objective to prevent harmful gender stereotypes.

Guy Parker, Chief Executive of the Advertising Standards Authority, said:

"Our evidence shows how harmful gender stereotypes in ads can contribute to inequality in society, with costs for all of us. Put simply, we found that some portrayals in ads can, over time, play a part in limiting people's potential. It's in the interests of women and men, our economy and society that advertisers steer clear of these outdated portrayals, and we're pleased with how the industry has already begun to respond."

14 June 2019

First ads banned for contravening UK gender stereotyping rules

Watchdog bans VW and Philadelphia ads with bungling dads and 'passive' women.

By Mark Sweney

Two television ads, one featuring new dads bungling comically while looking after their babies and the other a woman sitting next to a pram, have become the first to be banned under new rules designed to reduce gender stereotyping.

The Advertising Standards Authority (ASA) banned the ads for Philadelphia cream cheese and Volkswagen, following complaints from the public that they perpetuated harmful stereotypes.

The new rules, introduced at the beginning of the year, ban the depiction of men and women engaged in gender-stereotypical activities to help stop 'limiting how people see themselves and how others see them and the life decisions they take'.

In the ad for Philadelphia, the Mondelez-owned cream cheese brand, two new dads were shown eating lunch at a restaurant where food circulated on a conveyor belt. While chatting they accidentally find their babies are whisked away on it. "Let's not tell mum," one of them says.

Complainants said the tongue-in-cheek ad perpetuated a harmful stereotype suggesting men were incapable of caring for children and would put them at risk as a result of their incompetence.

Mondelez told the ASA it was stuck in a no-win situation, having specifically chosen two dads to avoid depicting the stereotypical image of showing two new mums handling all the childcare responsibilities.

The ASA banned the ad, saying it reinforced the idea that men were ineffective childcarers.

The ad for Volkswagen's electric eGolf vehicle showed a series of scenes including a man and a woman in a tent on a sheer cliff face, two male astronauts, a male para-athlete and a woman sitting on a bench next to a pram. Text stated: 'When we learn to adapt we can achieve anything.'

Complainants said the ad showed men engaged in adventurous activities, that unlike her male counterpart, the female rock climber was 'passive' because she was asleep, and that the woman with the pram was depicted in a stereotypical care-giving role.

Volkswagen said its ad was not sexist and that caring for a newborn was a life-changing experience about adaptation, regardless of the gender of the parent depicted.

The ASA, however, 'concluded that the ad presented gender stereotypes in a way that was likely to cause harm'.

Critics said the new rules were too draconian and that banning even the most innocuous use of gender stereotypes showed the watchdog had gone too far.

"It is concerning to see the ASA take on the role of the morality police," said Geraint Lloyd-Taylor, an advertising expert at the law firm Lewis Silkin. "It has let its zeal to enforce the new rules override its common sense in this first batch of rulings.

"The ASA seems to be out of sync with society in general. As it stands, the ASA's definition of 'harm' is unworkable and urgently needs to be clarified. I hope that these advertisers seek an independent review of the latest decisions."

Clearcast, the body responsible for vetting ads before they are broadcast, also expressed its frustration at the decisions. "We are naturally disappointed," it said. "The ASA's interpretation of the ads against the new rule and guidance goes further than we anticipated and has implications for a wide range of ads."

13 August 2019

www.theguardian.com

Toxic masculinity leaves most young men feeling pressurised to 'man up'

55 per cent said crying in front of others would make them feel like less of a man.

By Olivia Petter

More than half (61 per cent) of Britain's young men feel pressured to 'man up' as a result of damaging gender stereotypes, new research from YouGov reveals.

According to the findings, 67 per cent of 18–24-year-olds felt compelled to display 'hyper-masculine' behaviour in tough situations and 55 per cent said crying in front of others would make them feel like less of a man.

The survey, named Future Men, sheds light on the prevalence of archaic attitudes towards male identity and also revealed that very few people associate masculinity with positive traits.

For example, just one per cent of the 2,058 adults surveyed associated the term with honesty and only three per cent associated it with kindness.

One of the most dated stereotypes surrounding men and women is that the latter are more emotional while the former are stoic – but even this was found to be a prevalent attitude among those surveyed, with 53 per cent of young men saying they feel like society expects them to never ask for emotional support.

"To be masculine is often associated with being boorish, aggressive, inconsiderate and sometimes violent," says Christopher Muwanguzi, CEO of Working With Men, the charity who commissioned the survey for International Men's Day.

Muwanguzi tells *The Independent* that these links are instilled from a young age.

"We see it as early as the toddler years, when a boy who falls down, is told not to cry and to be a 'man' versus the girl that is comforted."

He went on to explain how important it is to tackle these attitudes if we're to address some of the worrying statistics surrounding men, such as suicide being the biggest killer of men under 45.

"Men are often expected to man up when faced with challenges, even when tackling serious mental health issues or complex problems. This means that many of them will not ask for help early enough, reinforcing the tradition of men asking for help when it's often too late."

He added that a call to action is needed now more than ever, particularly one year on from #MeToo, the global movement encouraging victims of sexual assault and harassment to speak out.

"By helping young men and boys understand that they don't have to conform to archaic aggressive stereotypes of masculinity, we hope to reduce antisocial behaviour, mental health struggles, suicides, gender-based crime and domestic violence."

20 November 2018

Why are we still designing pink toys for girls?

As Christmas approaches, designers, manufacturers and retailers should stop reinforcing outdated gender stereotypes by giving glittery unicorns to girls and dinosaurs to boys, and opt for gender-neutral products instead.

By Sara Jones

With Christmas just days away, I am in the throes of last-minute Christmas shopping.

Among the items that still need to be bought is a top for an eight-year-old, my youngest daughter. But I am struggling.

As I trawl through major UK department stores' online offerings, all I see are sparkly horses, glittery unicorns, sequin cats, shiny angels and pretty ballerinas. Yet none of these – nor anything sporting the ubiquitous 'Princess' slogan or, to be honest, that's pink – are her style or taste.

Not so long ago, John Lewis was introducing gender-neutral clothing and doing away with boys' and girls' labels. In the US, Target was launching gender-inclusive kids' clothing and home goods. And Swedish company Toca Boca's playful toys and apps designed with diversity and inclusivity in mind were grabbing headlines.

But things seem to have changed. In recent weeks, The Ultimate Kitchen Playset – a must-have Barbie accessory from Mattel in, yes, you've guessed it, bright pink – has become one of the bestsellers this Christmas, after being listed by a Toy Retailers Association panel as a 'top 12 dream Christmas toy'.

And while John Lewis may no longer put gender labels on toys – which is a big tick for them – it is selling Barbie's Ultimate Kitchen this Christmas, its website still lists 'girls' clothes' and 'boys' clothes', and when it comes to offering up glittery unicorns for girls and dinosaurs for boys, it is one of the worst offenders.

Go into any children's department at the moment and you will find boys' tops featuring astronauts, space rockets, dinosaurs, sharks, robots, guitars, cars, slogans like 'King of the World' and 'Winner!' and a largely blue colour palette – all of which is very much more to my daughter's taste.

So, what's the problem, you may well be thinking? Just buy your girl a boy's top. But counter-arguments such as these miss an important point.

Gendered products – from their basic design through to their packaging, graphics and branding – strengthens restrictive and outdated ideas.

And the biggest and most pernicious stereotype is that, while girls should aspire to be a sparkly, pretty princess whose only job is to be saved by Prince Charming, boys should dream of being action men and having adventures.

The heavy gendering of kids' stuff sends out restrictive messages to impressionable young children. Children should be free to choose whatever interests them, not what fits in a box of what these stereotypes dictate. Yes, girls – and boys – can choose 'girly' things if they want, but when they are affronted with so many pink and glittery items, there is very little choice.

By pushing the pink button, Mattel is exclusively targeting young girls and subliminally telling them that women should be doing the cooking – in my view, a sexist and out-of-date stereotype that toy manufacturers should be looking to disregard, rather than perpetuate.

True, this is the same company that previously released Barbie the vet, Barbie the scientist, Barbie the robotics engineer and Barbie the builder. But making the kitchen pink has sent Barbie back in time to 1950s style domestic servitude.

The trouble is that while there are some niche brands out there who are bravely trying to address the issue with more unisex options – brands like Tootsa MacGinty and Scamp & Dude – gender neutrality in product design, packaging and branding isn't yet infiltrating the mainstream.

There is, I believe, a socio-political and socio-economic reason for this. Consider the rapid upsurge in nostalgia that followed the financial crash in 2008 – a clear and unapologetic harking back by ordinary people to simpler, more straightforward times. And since then, nostalgia in design, marketing and advertising has become an effective way to build reassurance in uncertain times – the equivalent of comfort food.

The rise of the 'Keep Calm And Carry On' logo and its variations, for example, evoked the Blitz spirit by mythologising the good old days when everyone in Britain kept a stiff upper lip (despite the fact that most people were utterly miserable and life was pretty awful).

The recent glut of popular period TV dramas such as Call *The Midwife*, *Vanity Fair*, *Poldark*, *The Crown* and *Victoria* and even the cosy, gingham-and-check world of *The Great British Bake Off*, recall a supposedly softer, gentler 'golden era'.

Then there are our shops, filled with handcrafted this, bespoke that, and rustic the other.

We're buying vinyl records again and even cassettes are having a mini resurgence.

It's now a decade since the crash, of course. But we have President Trump, Brexit and the political, economic and social sense of chaos that has come about as a direct result of both. Is it any wonder, then, that we're choosing to wrap ourselves in a mirage of nostalgia to escape today's reality?

Which is what I believe is happening with children's products. In an attempt to reassure and engage, manufacturers and their marketers are harking back to a time that never really existed – a time when girls just wore pink and boys just wore blue.

Now let's be clear, it's not that I dislike pink. Nor do I think that we should neutralise colours of clothing and toys per se, because the more bland or neutral their colour (black, beiges and grey) the more it is, ironically, seen as male. But I do believe that there should be no 'right' or 'wrong' colours when it comes to gender, just as there should be no 'right' or 'wrong' interests or careers.

So I am still dreaming of a gender-neutral-coloured Christmas. Maybe next year.

20 December 2018

www.designweek.co.uk

Barbie manufacturer Mattel unveils 'gender inclusive' toy line that is 'free of labels'

The Creatable World dolls come with two hairstyle option – long or short – and can be dressed in trousers, a skirt or both.

Barbie manufacturer Mattel has unveiled a line of 'gender inclusive' dolls that its creators say will 'knock down barriers to play' and enable all children to 'express themselves freely'.

Named Creatable World, the line consists of six 'customisable' dolls available in different skin tones. The dolls are sold in kits containing two wigs and a selection of clothing and accessories, allowing children to style the toys with short or long hair, and a skirt, trousers, or both.

Mattel is best known for propelling Barbie to international stardom and in 2018 alone the 60-year-old clotheshorse generated in excess of US $1 billion (£800 milllion) in sales for the company. But some consumers have tired of the plastic plaything, accusing it of promoting unrealistic expectations about beauty and reinforcing sexist stereotypes among girls – a talking iteration launched in the Nineties issued proclamations including 'Math class is tough' and 'Want to go shopping?'

The US toymaker has attempted to tackle these concerns by launching pilot and engineer Barbies. It has also reacted to criticism around the lack of racial diversity in Barbie World by introducing a black doll with natural hair who uses a wheelchair, and subsequently a Rosa Parks figurine in honour of the civil rights activist.

Creatable World dolls 'free of labels'

The new Creatable World dolls, which retail at £34.99 each, were developed in consultation with parents, doctors and children, and have won praise from gender equality campaigners who viewed the range prior to its launch.

"We felt it was time to create a doll line free of labels," said Kim Culmone, senior vice president of design for Barbie and fashion dolls at Mattel.

"Through research, we heard that kids don't want their toys dictated by gender norms. This line allows all kids to express themselves freely... We're hopeful Creatable World will encourage people to think more broadly about how all kids can benefit from doll play."

The Creatable World range consists of six dolls with different skin tones. Cara Natterson a US paediatrician who consulted with Mattel during the toy's development, said she was asked to advise the manufacturer on what would be appropriate in terms of the size, proportions and physiology.

"A collection like this just knocks down every barrier to play," she said.

A toy for all children?

Megan Perryman campaigns with the UK grassroots group Let Toys Be Toys, which encourages retailers to stop categorising toys, books and clothes by gender and promoting some as suitable only for girls and others only for boys.

She believes 'children will see themselves reflected in the doll'.

"All children will feel that they can play with it," said Ms Perryman, a teacher.

"They won't feel put off by any marketing images, there's no colour or language or motifs that might suggest that Creatable World is for one child and not for another."

25 September 2019

www.inews.co.uk

How challenging masculine stereotypes is good for men

THE CONVERSATION

***An article from* The Conversation.**

By Michelle Stratemeyer, Associate Lecturer, School of Psychological Sciences, University of Melbourne

A man sits in a doctor's office after months of his wife's increasingly desperate pleas for him to seek professional help for his constant coughing. In the end, she was the one who booked his appointment and even drove him there.

Another man is meeting with his manager, anticipating derision and mockery when he mentions he needs to reduce his workload to accommodate the birth of his first child.

A third man has a violent encounter outside a pub, fuelled by binge drinking and machismo. He cops a blow to the head and crumples, hitting his head against the pavement.

These aren't just stereotypes of men. They are the types of experiences and outcomes that reliably differ between men and women. Men are 32% less likely to visit a health professional than women. Men are also less likely to seek therapy for psychological complaints, such as feeling down or anxious.

Men also experience higher rates of suicide and motor accidents, are more likely to drink excessively and smoke, and are more prone to serious health conditions such as heart attacks, strokes and vascular disease.

Similarly, men are more likely to both perpetrate and experience violence, and to adopt beliefs and behaviours that increase the risk of violence.

It is no surprise that men die four years earlier, on average, than women. A woman can expect to live to just over 84, while a man can expect to live to just over 80.

In a bid to improve men's health and well-being, the American Psychological Association (APA) recently released guidelines for psychologists when working with boys and men.

These guidelines complement the APA's 2007 guidelines for working with girls and women. Both guidelines share commonalities, such as focusing on gender-appropriate therapeutic practices and education.

The APA is acknowledging that gender issues are relevant to everyone, not just women, and that the experiences of men may differ to those of women.

But despite the positive intentions of the guidelines, their release was met by backlash and unfounded criticisms in some parts of the media.

What do the guidelines actually say?

The guidelines aim to challenge some aspects of traditional masculinity that might cause problems in men's lives.

Traditional masculinity encompasses a set of norms, ideas and beliefs about what it means to be a man. Such beliefs include identifying men as self-reliant, emotionally reticent, focused on work over family, and oversexed.

When these beliefs are taken to an extreme level, they can result in poor outcomes for men, such as being dissatisfied in romantic relationships, having mental health problems, and engaging in more risky behaviours.

To illustrate the impact of these traditional ideas of masculinity on men's health and wellbeing, let's look at three of the ten APA recommendations in detail.

First, the guidelines urge psychologists to address the high rates of problems like violence, substance abuse and suicide, which are more commonly experienced by men.

The guidelines highlight the link between beliefs about traditional forms of masculinity and the encouragement of aggressive behaviour in boys by family, peers and the media.

As a result, men are more likely to display violent behaviours and to be victims of violence.

The guidelines also highlight the negative links between male childhood abuse and victimisation, and later aggressive behaviour, suicidal thoughts and substance abuse.

Recognising these patterns offers an opportunity for therapists to engage in gender-appropriate conversations and tailor behavioural change to the problems that plague men.

Second, the guidelines highlight the importance of encouraging men's positive involvement in families.

Despite increasing numbers of dual-income households, there is still strong social pressure for men to be the providers and breadwinners rather than taking on nurturing and caring roles. This expectation can come at the expense of men's relationships with their partners, children and extended family.

Encouraging men's positive involvement with their families has been shown to improve health and well-being outcomes for men, their children and their partners.

It may have spillover benefits in making work practices more progressive, with better balance between paid work and time spent with loved ones.

Third, the guidelines highlight the need for boys and men to more willingly seek help and health care.

Men are more likely than women to die from diseases such as colorectal cancer, which can be prevented with the right health care.

In terms of mental health, men's reluctance to express emotions and seek help through therapy may underlie the high rates of self-harm and suicide.

Traditional masculinity also encourages risky and competitive actions in men, resulting in unintentional injuries being the leading cause of death in men under 45.

According to the guidelines, we need to shift beliefs around self-reliance so men feel more comfortable looking after themselves and seeking professional help and services when needed.

Taken together, the APA guidelines have the potential to improve the lives of men. The guidelines squarely focus on the disparities in outcomes between men and women, and provide clear suggestions on improving men's well-being through strategies like strengthening family engagement and changing attitudes towards embracing healthy behaviours.

Many non-profit organisations and advocacy groups are already taking on this challenge to encourage healthy masculinity among boys and men. Our Watch, Australia's national foundation to prevent violence against women and their children, for instance, provides resources and articles for young people on masculinity and what it means to be a man through their campaign, The Line.

By recognising that gender also affects men, we can move towards improving the way that clinicians, practitioners and society support boys and men.

27 March 2019

www.theconversation.com

Key Facts

- International Women's Day began in 1911. (page 1)
- Women are 47% more likely to suffer severe injuries in car crashes because safety features are designed for men. (page 1)
- Only 6 countries give women equal legal work rights as men. (page 2)
- The United Nations Foundation estimates that 62 million girls worldwide are denied the basic human right of affordable and accessible education. (page 6)
- At least 200 million girls and women alive today have had their genitals mutilated – suffering one of the most inhuman acts of gender-based violence in the world. (page 7)
- The Representation of the People Act was given Royal Assent from George V on 6 February 1918, giving approximately 8.4 million women the vote. (page 10)
- Before 1870, married women were required to relinquish all property and earnings to their husbands, effectively giving them the same legal status as an insane person or a criminal. (page 10)
- The Sex Discrimination Act 1975 made it illegal to discriminate against women in work, education and training. It also meant women could apply for a credit card or loan in their own name. (page 12)
- In 2017, 4,382 men took their own lives, an average of 12 per day. In comparison, 1,439 women died by suicide in the same time frame: about four per day. (page 18)
- According to data from UCAS, in 2017 over 71,000 less men were accepted to UK universities than women. In the class of 2017, men make up around 43% of new freshers. (page 19)
- Homelessness is an issue which disproportionately affects men. A 2017 study from the Ministry of Housing, Communities and Social Affairs found that 86% of rough sleepers are men. (page 20)
- A study by Ipsos Mori, in collaboration with the Global Institute for Women's Leadership at King's College London and International Women's Day, has found that while a third of British men think they are being expected to do too much to support women's equality, far more – half – do not. In fact, three in five men in Britain agree that gender equality won't be achieved unless they also take action to support women's rights. (page 22)
- Seeing parental behaviours are more influential than parental attitudes when children are developing their own attitudes towards gender equality. (page 23)
- Female consumers pay on average 60 pence more per 10ml of fragrance than male shoppers, suggesting the existence of a Pink Tax on perfume, according to data published by a price comparison site. (page 24)
- Women gamers face roughly three times more harassment than men when playing online. (page 25)
- Stereotyping in childhood has wide-ranging and significant negative consequences for both women and men, with more than half (51%) of people affected saying it constrained their career choices and 44% saying it harmed their personal relationships. (page 28)
- 69% of men aged under 35 said that gender stereotyping of children has a damaging effect on perceptions of what it means to be a man or a woman. (page 28)
- According to the *Global Gender Gap Index*, 108 years are needed to close the global gender gap. (page 30)
- A 2016 survey of more than 30,000 employees found that women who negotiated for promotions were 30% more likely than men to be labelled intimidating, bossy or aggressive. (page 31)
- A new rule in the Advertising Codes was introduced by CAP and ASA at the beginning of 2019. The rule bans the depiction of men and women engaged in gender-stereotypical activities to help stop 'limiting how people see themselves and how others see them and the life decisions they take'. (page 33)
- More than half (61 per cent) of Britain's young men feel pressured to 'man up' as a result of damaging gender stereotypes, new research from YouGov reveals. (page 34)
- 67 per cent of 18–24–year–olds felt compelled to display 'hyper-masculine' behaviour in tough situations and 55 per cent said crying in front of others would make them feel like less of a man. (page 34)
- Men are 32% less likely to visit a health professional than women. Men are also less likely to seek therapy for psychological complaints, such as feeling down or anxious. (page 38)
- Men die four years earlier, on average, than women. A woman can expect to live to just over 84, while a man can expect to live to just over 80. (page 38)

ASA (Advertising Standards Authority)

An independent regulatory body for monitoring advertising across broadcast and non-broadcast media.

Equality Act 2010

This Act brings a number of existing laws together in one place. It sets out the personal characteristics that are protected by law, and behaviour which is unlawful. The 'protected characteristics' are age; disability; gender reassignment; marriage and civil partnership; pregnancy and maternity; race; religion and belief; sex and sexual orientation. Under the Act people are not allowed to discriminate against, harass or victimise another person because they have any of the protected characteristics.

Feminism

Advocating women's rights and equality between the sexes.

FGM (female genital mutilation)

A harmful procedure where the female genitals are deliberately cut, injured or changed. There are no medical reasons for this to be done.

Gender

Gender is sexual identity, especially in relation to society or culture; the condition of being female or male. Gender refers to socially-constructed roles, learned behaviours and expectations associated with females and males. Gender is more than just biology: it is the understanding we gain from society and those around us of what it means to be a girl/woman or a boy/man.

Gender bias

A preference or prejudice toward one gender over the other. Can be conscious or unconscious.

Gender neutral

A term not referrring to either sex but referring to people in general.

Gender stereotypes

Simplifying the roles, attributes and differences between males and females. Gender stereotyping encourages children to behave in ways that are considered most typical of their sex. For example, buying pink toys for girls and blue for boys, or limiting girls to playing with dolls and boys to toy cars.

Glass ceiling

The term 'glass ceiling' refers to the problem of an invisible 'barrier' that prevents someone from progressing in their career to upper-level positions. Particularly for women and minorities.

Pay gap

The gender pay gap refers to the difference between men and women's earnings. Currently, women earn on average 21% less than their male counterparts.

Pink tax

The term 'pink tax' refers to the extra money women are charged for certain products or services above the standard cost for comparable goods aimed at men; often these items are coloured pink to indicate they have been developed for female consumers.

Sex/gender discrimination

Treating someone differently because they are male, female or transgendered, resulting in a disadvantage to them in a certain area of life, e.g. employment, education.

Sexual abuse

Sexual abuse occurs when a victim is forced into a sexual act against their will, through violence or intimidation. This can include rape. Sexual abuse is always a crime, no matter what the relationship is between the victim and perpetrator.

Sexual bullying/harassment

This includes a range of behaviours such as sexualised name-calling and verbal abuse, mocking someone's sexual performance, ridiculing physical appearance, criticising sexual behaviour, spreading rumours about someone's sexuality or about sexual experiences they have had or not had, unwanted touching and physical assault. Sexual bullying is behaviour which is repeated over time and intends to victimise someone by using their gender, sexuality or sexual (in)experience to hurt them.

Suffragette

A woman who campaigned for the right of women to vote in the early part of the 20th century.

Toxic masculinity

A cultural concept of manliness that glorifies stoicism, strength, virility and dominance, and that is socially maladaptive or harmful to mental health.

Activities

Brainstorming

In small groups, discuss what you know about gender equality. Consider the following points:

- What does the term 'gender equality' mean?
- List as many things as you can think of that are 'unequal' between men and women.
- List all the things you can think of that are 'equal' between men and women.
- How and where do we learn our perception of male and female roles?
- Can you give an example of a situation where you feel you have been discriminated against because of your gender?

Research

- In our current government, how many female MPs have a seat in the Houses of Parliament? Do some online research to find out. Compare this figure with the stats from four other European countries' governments.
- Choose a country other than your own and, using the Internet, do some research to find out about gender equality in that country. Write some notes on your findings and feedback to your class.
- Look at the article and graphs on pages 8 and 9 – which key area of gender inequality do British people think is the most pressing issue that needs to be addressed?
- Visit a local bookshop and go to the children's section. Is there a clear divide between the books aimed at girls and the books aimed at boys? How can you tell if a book is aimed at boys rather than girls? Is there a 'gender neutral' section? Make some notes on your findings and share with your class.

Design

- Design a poster promoting:
  - International Men's Day (19 November), or
  - International Women's Day (8 March).
- Thinking about how gender stereotypes have been used in advertising in the past, find an example of an old advert from the 1970s or 1980s. Redesign the advert for a modern audience. What changes have you had to make so the ad would not contravene the new UK Advertising Codes that have recently come into force.
- Choose one of the articles in this book and create an illustration to highlight the key themes/message of your chosen article.
- As a class, watch the film *Suffragette* (2015) starring Carey Mulligan and Helena Bonham Carter. Either:
  - Design a poster to promote the film; or,
  - Imagine you were part of the Suffrage movement over a century ago and design a poster persuading women to join the cause.
- In recent years, practicality, equality and inclusivity have been big issues surrounding school uniforms (see the article on page 13). Look at your school or college's uniform policy – what do you agree/disagree with? In small groups, design a new uniform for your school that you believe is fair and inclusive. Compare with the designs of the other groups in your class.

Oral

- "We shouldn't fight for 'gender equality'. We should fight to abolish gender," Debate this motion as a class, with one group arguing in favour and the other against.
- Divide your class into two halves. One half should discuss male stereotypes and the other should discuss female stereotypes. Create a poster to demonstrate your ideas and then share with the rest of your class.
- As a class, discuss whether you believe men should be the primary 'breadwinners' of the household.
- In 2018, Jodie Whittaker became the first female actor to fill the role of The Doctor in the long-running and popular British television sci-fi series *Doctor Who*. Her appointment as the Thirteenth Doctor met with some controversy. Thinking about TV, films and literature, discuss other fictional characters you would like to see portrayed as the opposite of their presented gender. Can you name any popular gender-neutral fictional characters?
- Look at the *Landmark dates for women* timeline on page 11. In small groups, discuss what would you most like to see next added to that list.

Reading/writing

- Read the novel *A Handmaid's Tale* by Margaret Atwood, or, watch HBO's TV adaptation of the book. It's the story of a future dystopia in which women are virtually enslaved in accordance with an extreme interpretation of Old Testament morality. Write a review, focusing on how the book/TV series portrays notions of gender and identity through the character of Offred.
- Write a one-paragraph definition of gender equality.
- Choose one of the illustrations from throughout this book and write 300 words exploring the themes the artist has chosen to depict.

Index

Acknowledgements

The publisher is grateful for permission to reproduce the material in this book. While every care has been taken to trace and acknowledge copyright, the publisher tenders its apology for any accidental infringement or where copyright has proved untraceable. The publisher would be pleased to come to a suitable arrangement in any such case with the rightful owner.

Images

Cover image courtesy of iStock. All other images courtesy of Freepik, Pixabay and Unsplash.

Illustrations

Don Hatcher: pages 28 & 35. Simon Kneebone: pages 23 & 30. Angelo Madrid: pages 5 & 27.

Additional acknowledgements

With thanks to the Independence team: Shelley Baldry, Danielle Lobban, Jackie Staines and Jan Sunderland.

Tracy Biram

Cambridge, January 2020